THE PEANUT BUTTER
Man

SO-AGZ-102

for TEAM's library in Wheaton

Russ Irwin
Col / 28

THE PEANUT BUTT ER

Man

Russ Irwin

PLEASE RETURN TO
BRANSON RESOURCE CENTER
P.O. BOX 909
WHEATON IL 60187

TATE PUBLISHING & *Enterprises*

The Peanut Butter Man
Copyright © 2010 by Russ Irwin. All rights reserved.

No part of this publication may be reproduced, stored in a retrieval system or transmitted in any way by any means, electronic, mechanical, photocopy, recording or otherwise without the prior permission of the author except as provided by USA copyright law.

Scripture taken from the *Holy Bible, New International Version*®. NIV®. Copyright© 1973, 1978, 1984 by International Bible Society. Used by permission of Zondervan. All rights reserved.

The opinions expressed by the author are not necessarily those of Tate Publishing, LLC.

Published by Tate Publishing & Enterprises, LLC
127 E. Trade Center Terrace | Mustang, Oklahoma 73064 USA
1.888.361.9473 | www.tatepublishing.com

Tate Publishing is committed to excellence in the publishing industry. The company reflects the philosophy established by the founders, based on Psalm 68:11,
"The Lord gave the word and great was the company of those who published it."

Book design copyright © 2010 by Tate Publishing, LLC. All rights reserved.
Cover design by Amber Gulilat
Interior design by Jeff Fisher

Published in the United States of America

ISBN: 978-1-61566-726-0
Biography & Autobiography, Religious
10.01.26

THE PEANUT BUTTER MAN

Mehmood Shah Qureshi (1923–1999) was saved from a religion of works to eternal life in Jesus Christ. He experienced many hardships along the bumpy road that followed, but with each bump he found the words of Jesus Christ to be true: "My grace is sufficient for you."

He was a strict follower of a religion and had every intention of staying with that religion all the days of his life,

"But God ..."

God had other plans, plans that were far better than he could have imagined.

DEDICATION

I dedicate this to my wife, Phyllis, who has been my faithful life companion for fifty-seven years. She has been a wonderful mother to our three children and cared for them and myself in spite of carrying on heavy responsibilities at TEAM's mission hospital in the foothills of the Himalayas in northern Pakistan.

She paved the path of book writing in our family when she authored *Doctor Memsahib,* an interesting account of being a missionary doctor and mother at the same time. Her persistence in her first experience as an author served as a steadying factor for me, when I reached obstacles in writing and wondered if it was worth the effort to overcome them.

ACKNOWLEDGMENTS

The author was so dependent on information from others that he served more as a compiler of this book than its author. The following contributed so much content to this biography. They saw sides of Qureshi's life with which the author was not so well acquainted.

Bill Dalton, a valued counselor for Qureshi in his early Christian life. The promoter of the peanut butter idea for Qureshi.

Jonathan Mitchell, acquainted with Qureshi from childhood, but who carried on a close friendship with Qureshi after his own parents retired from their work in Pakistan.

David and Synnove Mitchell, very close friends and encouragers of the Qureshi family for many years.

Denis Sherbeck, who—with David Mitchell—made a video recording of Mr. and Mrs. Qureshi as they jointly recorded their story for posterity.

Jean Sodemann, who did much of the transcribing and editing of the video.

Don Stoddard, who encouraged Qureshi in various stages of his Christian life.

The following offered valuable suggestions during the editing process:

Ruth Nygren Keller, a missionary kid who grew up in Pakistan

Cindy Irwin, the author's daughter

Phyllis Irwin, the author's wife

Patty McGarvey, the author's older daughter

The following, in addition to the author, contributed pictures:

Bob Blanchard

David Mitchell

Jonathan Mitchell

TABLE OF
CONTENTS

INTRODUCTION

God's sovereignty is so evident throughout creation, yet when it comes to His being in charge with more of our personal lives than we would prefer, it is easy to dismiss the thought and carry on business as usual in our own strength and wisdom. Qureshi's story demonstrates many times not only God's sovereignty, but also the wisdom of bowing to him, confessing that he knows what's best at all times for us his children.

To make as clear as possible God's complete control in Qureshi's life, the two words "But God ..." are used many times in this story. These two words are found forty-three times in the King James Version; sixty-one times in the New International Version; and sixty times in the New Living Translation.

The reader would do well to look back in his own life and acknowledge the many times God has exercised his sovereignty in his own life.

In this story you will be introduced to many facets of Pakistani life: how individual decisions must be made in consultation with family leaders, marrying first cousins, marriage customs, educating children from very young age in ways of Islam, the two main sects of Islam, etc.

It is the wish of the author that each person who becomes acquainted with Qureshi and his family will be encouraged to be as bold as Qureshi in being an ambassador for the Lord Jesus Christ.

THE GAS CAP SAGA

One bright spring morning, a teen-age boy came running up to me, almost tripping over his own feet. He obviously had a juicy bit of information to share.

"The missionaries ..." he breathlessly blurted out, "the missionaries have set up camp near the railway station! We know why they are there. They plan to teach the Bible in the few Christian homes they can find, but they will also make visits in Muslim homes in order to persuade our people to change their religion. We should never allow that!"

I quickly picked up on my duty as the son of a religious leader, an *imam*, and warned this young man and his buddies, "Thanks for the information, but listen you guys, don't listen to that Christian stuff. We have our own holy book and Allah's holy prophet Mohammed (peace be upon him). Don't waste time on that foolishness. Most of you are not strong enough in your own belief as yet. You could become prey to their false teaching." As they walked away, I was pleased that their facial expressions showed they understood my warning.

A few days later one of the young men hatched up a plan.

He confided in his buddies: "Hey, let's take the gas cap from the missionary's car and then"—his eyes narrowed menacingly—"we'll pour sand and dirt into his gas tank. He won't get far after that." They couldn't wait to carry out their sinister plan; they were sure their scheme would teach the missionary a lesson, so he would stop trying to convert Muslims. And as a bonus they hoped for a commendation from the *imam*.

Because I had also spoken so strongly against the missionary activities, one of the culprits knocked at my door and informed me with a smirk on his face about their action. His face was full of expectation, as he showed me the gas cap. Unfortunately for him, I didn't respond as he had hoped.

Qureshi before knowing joy in Jesus

"How dare you do such a thing!" I retorted. "Even though their message conflicts with that of the Holy Quran, these people are guests in our country. Give me that gas cap!"

Because of my unexpected and angry response the boy turned and ran away with the cap. I jumped on my bicycle, caught up with him, and scolded him. When the boy heard the tone of my voice, he quickly pulled the gas cap out of his pocket, threw it down, and hurriedly jumped over a nearby wall to escape my wrath.

I grabbed the gas cap and biked toward the railway station, expecting to find their car stalled somewhere in those four miles, but it was nowhere to be seen. When I reached the station I spotted their car near the four tents they had set up. As I approached the largest one, a servant appeared.

"I would like to meet the man in charge," I said, still trying to catch my breath.

The servant tugged on a wire outside the tent. A brass bell jingled inside, and a very cordial Willie Sutherland emerged. He shook my hand warmly and beckoned me in. Upon hearing that I was from Pind Sultani, he assumed I had come to learn about Christianity. His expression changed suddenly, as I removed the gas cap from my pocket.

"Sir, I have come to return your gas cap."

With a look of bewilderment, Willie took the gas cap and headed for the car. He stuck his finger into the pipe leading to the gas tank and was shocked to find it packed with sand and dirt. Immediately he instructed his helper to jack up the back of the car and take the tank off.

As his helper cleaned the tank, Willie thanked me profusely and invited me into the tent. After the usual cup of sweet milk tea, I started to leave. As a parting gift, Willie handed me some literature. I glanced at it and accepted it only out of respect for the foreigner. If certain people found me with Christian literature, rumors could spread. That would reflect on the honor of my father who was the *imam* in our village.

I took the literature and gave a slight nod of gratitude. As an afterthought, I asked for Willie's address and wrote it on a small piece of paper. As I turned to leave, he added, "If you have any questions about these booklets, feel free to come to my house anytime. I live near the jail in Attock City. Everyone knows where that is."

After returning home in the evening, I detailed the day's events for my uncle and others in the family and showed them the pamphlets.

"The sahib handed me these as I was leaving." The titles of the pamphlets caught the attention of my relatives: "Some Wrong Perceptions," "Abolished," and "Changed." They surmised the pamphlets had something to do with the Christian's holy book.

Looking over the pamphlets, we were surprised to find references to the Quran as well as to the Bible. The pamphlets were interesting, but at the same time confusing. When talking about the Bible they used words and numbers that meant nothing to us: for example, "John chapter 5" or "James chapter 2."

I wrote these phrases on a piece of paper and stuck it in my pocket. This happened to be the same piece of paper on which I had written Willie's address. Although I really had no interest in the Christian literature, for some reason that piece of paper remained in my pocket for many weeks. Little did I realize that God's sovereignty was at work even in this seemingly insignificant matter.

✝

A few months later I was in Attock City regarding registration papers for some land. As I left the lawyer's office, I remembered that piece of paper. I fumbled through things in my pocket and finally found it: "Mission House, Jail Road."

I asked for directions and soon realized that about everyone knew where the missionary lived. Willie was just leaving to attend the Sunday morning church service. As he emerged from the compound gate, he saw me out of the corner of his eye and stopped. He greeted me with his usual smile and friendly hug. Right off the bat he asked, "I'm leaving for our worship service. Why don't you come along?" Curiosity overcame reluctance, so I consented to go.

I found their way of "saying prayers" very interesting. People left their shoes outside as we Muslims do when entering a mosque, but it was strange to me that women and children also were in the meeting. I was pleased to see that ladies and children sat on one side of the room separate from the men.

Previously I had gone by their church building during their prayers and heard singing, but this time I could observe first hand what they did when they met. Many people knew the songs by heart, but several used well-worn songbooks. A man sitting near the front beat enthusiastically on a pair of tublas, which are short drums played while the drummer sits on the floor. Another musician used a harmonium. As he sang energetically, he also pumped the bellows with his left hand and played the keyboard with his right. These musicians were not as good as some of the entertainers I'd heard at weddings or had seen in movies from India, but they were okay for that group.

I braced myself for the speech that was to follow. Surprisingly, I heard nothing offensive about Islam as I expected. This was a contrast to sermons in mosques that can contain derogatory or scathing remarks about Christianity.

After the service, Willie and I walked the dusty path to his home. Over the whirling sound of the overhead fan hanging from the twenty-two-foot ceiling, we drank tea and chatted. However, I quickly got to the point, for I did not want Willie to have any misconceptions about the purpose of my visit.

I pulled the wrinkled piece of paper from my pocket.

"There were names and numbers in the pamphlets you gave me that meant nothing to us." With a puzzled look I asked, "Can you explain them?" Willie took a book from his desk and read from a couple places. I quickly asked, "What book is that?"

"It's the Holy Bible, which contains the books of Moses, David, and the teachings of Jesus Christ. It has the laws and commands God gave to the prophets. It also tells about heaven and hell. Best of all, it tells about God's great prophet Jesus Christ and what he has done so we can freely receive forgiveness of our sins."

"Freely receive forgiveness of sins?" That is very unusual, for there is nothing like that in Islam. The Quran teaches we have to strive very hard to have any hope of forgiveness."

"How much is this book?" I asked.

"We give it for an offering of four rupees."

I pulled two rupees from my pocket and added, "I'll give you the other two the next time I'm in Attock City." Willie broke into a smile.

"That's all right. You don't need to pay the rest. But should you have further questions, be sure to come back and ask me." At that point I asked permission to leave and rode off on my bicycle.

I took the Bible home, where it remained on a shelf, collecting dust. I do admit, however, that a few times I peeked at it out of curiosity, but primarily with the purpose of looking for changes Christians and Jews had made.

Several years later, a Christian shoemaker in my village somehow heard that I had an interest in the Bible. One day I was cycling through the market place, and he invited me into his small shop.

"I heard by the grapevine that you have shown some interest in the Bible. Have a cup of tea and let me tell you a bit about it. I'm not too well educated, but I know it's a very powerful book." As he continued working, he gave a brief synopsis of the Bible and explained the major theme of salvation from our sins, plus the new spiritual life that accompanies repentance and forgiveness.

As he talked I was flipping through pages of his Bible, taking time to glance at a verse here and there. Suddenly my eye fell on a verse that greatly puzzled me.

> He has blinded their eyes, and he hardened their heart, lest they see with their eyes and perceive with their heart, and be converted, and I heal them.
>
> John 12:40

This was confusing. It seemed to make God look like an ogre. Rather than spend time on it just then, I let the matter go.

My occasional looking into the Bible showed that the Moses, Noah, Adam, David, and Solomon of the Bible are the same as those mentioned in the Quran. However, when I opened the New Testament, I always remembered: "Christians have changed its message. Stay away from that book."

Even my wife warned me, "Don't read the book of that religion! Several people have been led astray by reading it."

"But God..."

God had plans for me that I knew nothing about. Up to this point I knew only the teachings of Islam. All I ever heard about Christianity were negative teachings, such as its three gods and that their God had a wife, Mary, and a son they called Jesus. I also heard that Christians believe they are forgiven for all their sins, past, present, and future. What a license for licentious living! This was not for me. Muslims have a much higher standard.

CHILDHOOD

Boys in our village were fond of field hockey and cricket, and the prize possession of fortunate boys was a cricket bat. In lieu of a regulation-size field, we played cricket in the alleys or any available level area. For a wicket we set up a tin can, a few small stones, or just whatever fit the need. Since my father was the *imam* in our village, he was more interested in my learning Islam than in my cricket skills. Therefore, I didn't play as much cricket as my neighbor boys.

The preparation for me to be a good Muslim started the day I was born.

An *imam* whispered in my ear soon after my umbilical cord was cut, "There is no God but Allah, and Mohammed is his prophet." I heard those words many times every day for the rest of my life. I heard them from the village mosques, from shops, in my school, and, most importantly, in my home. Even my name reflected the religion of my parents. My family name of Qureshi comes from the name of the Quresh tribe, from which the prophet Mohammad (570–632) and his wife, Aamina, both descended.

My father habitually used Allah's name many times every day. He began work, a meal, or travel with *Bismillah,* which means "in the name of Allah." When facing a danger, *Allah khair* automatically sprang from his lips. These two comforting words mean "May Allah make everything come out okay."

Each time he spoke of doing something in the future, he used the Arabic phrase *Insha'allah* ("If Allah wills"). Since God alone controls the future, my father was assured by this phrase. (Years later I learned that the Injeel, the New Testament, teaches the same thing in James 4:13–16.)

Through my father's invoking Allah's name so regularly and by his saying prayers very faithfully five times every day, I learned how important it was to be fully devoted to Almighty Allah. Not only did my father say his prayers five times a day, he also prepared for prayer each time with the required ablution. For this he washed out his mouth and ears using his index finger of his right hand to assure that each oral and aural crevice was clean. Then he washed his face, hands, and lower arms, as well as his feet and lower parts of his legs by pouring water over them. Even in winter, using cold water, he faithfully performed that ritual. By observing his faithfulness in religious duties, I knew that Islam was the most important part of my father's life. That also became true in my life. Until I was in my late thirties, it was the only religion I knew or wanted!

✝

I was born near Pind Sultani in January, 1917. This village is located about half way between the major cities of Islamabad and Peshawar. Nearly 99 percent of its population was Muslim, with just a few Christians living among us. Most of them were sweepers who kept our streets clean from droppings of horses, donkeys, water buffalo, and sheep.

Trips into Pind Sultani with my father were always a treat. Its dirt streets and alleyways usually were crowded with various kinds of traffic. Local farmers directed their heavily-laden donkeys through the maze of slow moving traffic. Water buffalo lazily pulled carts with supplies brought in from the countryside. On certain days farmers brought in herds of water buffalo, sheep, and goats into the village to sell or trade. Prospective buyers bickered with owners over prices. Meat dealers bought some of the animals and butchered them on the spot. They hung their freshly cut sections of beef, mutton, etc. on large hooks in front of their shops. The cries of hawkers, the braying of donkeys, and the cackling of numerous chickens added much to the cacophony of those shopping days. I enjoyed every minute of it.

✝

Each morning before daylight, I heard my father give the call to prayer from the local mosque. In all types of weather, he trudged up the steps of the prayer tower. After reaching the top and hesitating to catch his breath, he would throw back his bearded head and call the faithful to prayer with Arabic words 1400 years old:

> Come to prayer, come to salvation,
>
> Prayer is better than sleep.

As a boy I couldn't comprehend the need for such unearthly hours, but as I matured, I took real pride in emulating my father's faithfulness. He climbed those stone steps of the minaret each day, regardless of the weather. He gave the call five times daily; each call was different from the other four. Everyone in our village could recite all of them, for they had heard those calls every day of their entire lives.

The only time we ever heard Christians call their people to prayer was on Sunday mornings. And I thought, *What shirkers they must be! Not only in our village, but in every village and town in Pakistan, imams call Muslims to prayer thirty-five times each week. But Christians? Once is enough for a whole week! Phooey on them!*

In addition to being lackadaisical about their religion, I learned that Christians have several beliefs that we Muslims cannot believe:

1. Belief in three gods
2. Changed their holy book
3. Claim that God has a partner, which makes them worse than pagans
4. Claim that the Almighty Creator made himself into a man whom they call the Son of God
5. Claim God fathered a son with the Virgin Mary.

My conclusion? *How stupid these Christians must be.* These two religions are poles apart. I knew I could never have anything to do with such a corrupt religion.

✝

My father taught me to take responsibilities when I was quite young. For example, when I was in second grade, my father traveled abroad for a few weeks as a Muslim missionary. Before leaving he told me to find some jobs, so my mother and all of us children would have food to eat. Even though I was very young, I poured myself into this responsibility and looked into several possibilities for odd jobs. Some days I moved boxes from place to place at the railway station. In the evenings after school a local shopkeeper allowed me to help him. From these bits and pieces, and with Allah's blessings, we had enough to eat during my father's absence.

In my teen years, I was a bit cleverer. I thought of a way to earn a few quick rupees. Word had spread in the village that the tax collector was soon to be in town for his annual visit. I reasoned that if I got an official-looking notebook and could visit homes before he arrived, I could pocket some money. It didn't work! People in our village knew I had not been appointed as a tax collector, so they informed the police. I'll never forget the five days I shared with mice and lice in a dirty, lonely cell, so I could "contemplate my evil deed," as the police described it.

As the son of the *imam* it was important for the family honor that I become more serious about life as a Muslim. My time in jail was an embarrassment for my father, and he insisted that I make a complete turnaround. To accomplish his purpose he began giving me responsibilities in the mosque. I was the smartest of his students, so he felt comfortable in allowing me to lead the daily prayers when he was visiting other villages. What I enjoyed most was the chance to teach his classes when he was away!

I soon got in over my head, trying to pacify both Shias and Sunnis in class. The more orthodox view of the Sunnis conflicts with the more mystic side of the Shias. Sunnis strictly follow the teachings of the Quran. Shias, on the other hand, visit shrines to obtain favors from Allah and look to so-called holy men for guidance for such things as money, land, women, and healing. To minimize the differences between the two groups I emphasized the basics that both groups rigidly follow. This made for smoother classes. They all needed more teaching about the five pillars of Islam:

1. The creed: There is no God but Allah, and Mohammed is his prophet

2. Pray five times a day

3. Fast one lunar month each year

4. Give alms to the poor

5. Make the pilgrimage to Mecca, if means allow

Besides teaching the basics of Islam to my father's students, I also encouraged them to memorize large portions of the Quran. Since I had done this from youth, my example spurred them on.

The future seemed bright. I envisioned myself as becoming a popular and effective teacher of Islam like my father. I too would have chances to travel and teach other religious leaders. People would consult me for answers about religion, family problems, and other issues. Indeed the future was promising.

For me, Christianity was nowhere in sight. Actually, all I had heard about that religion repelled me from any attempt to understand it. One of my personal observations of Christians strengthened my abhorrence of their religion. A foreign family from the West, and therefore obviously Christian, was working on a large construction project a few miles from Attock City.

When one of their dogs died, they buried it near the edge of their courtyard and marked the grave with a stone. *A cemetery for dogs? What could be more absurd? Dogs in our religion are despised creatures.* I shrugged my shoulders and thought that somehow dogs must fit into the Christian religion. This new "insight" made me even more thankful that I was born a Muslim. I knew that nothing, absolutely nothing, could move me from that position.

Neither did I know the power of two small but very effective words in the Bible:

"But God…"

Fortunately, God did get my attention. It was by very small grains of sand. Later in life, I was forever grateful to God for allowing mischievous boys to put sand in Willie Sutherland's gas tank. Without that incident I could have remained forever in the throes of a religion that offers no assurance of heaven.

MARRIAGE AND THE ARMY

I was married in 1936, and I served in the army from 1939 to 1943. Due to a misunderstanding and my hot temper, I argued with a high-ranking Hindu army officer and actually cursed him. Soldiers do not treat officers this way, so I went to jail.

I had been married to Nur J'haan for six years, and God had blessed us with two daughters. At the time of my incarceration, my wife was carrying our third child and was due to give birth in a few days. What a terrible time to be separated from my wife and children!

During those lonely days behind bars, I received the earthshaking news that my wife had been in very difficult labor and died while giving birth. To add to this bitter experience, our baby died, too, and he was a boy! This was a blow! I was not able to see either the baby or my wife's body, or take part in the prayers at the funeral. The baby being a boy made it even more devastating, for, just like all Muslim fathers, I had wanted a son more than anything. In spite of my great sorrow, the police kept me behind bars.

My family did what they could to get me released, but to no avail. The army was about to court-martial me for my despicable remarks, so my family sold a cow and brought the cash to post bail. In my country, money talks very loudly, but the cash they raised did not budge the officer who had been insulted. That night I was so distraught that I cut strands from a rug and planned to hang myself.

"But God..."

A fellow prisoner saw what I was doing and persuaded me to get help instead of committing suicide. I listened to him and started to think of what else I could do. I suddenly remembered my missionary friend, Willie Sutherland, so I wrote him a letter.

Willie received the letter while far away in the hills of Mussoorie, India, but he answered immediately. His reply greatly encouraged me, for he promised to visit just as soon as he returned from vacation.

At the same time the Lord was working in another unexpected way. Incredibly, the commissioner who listened to my case was a kind and considerate person. After my lawyer presented my case again, the commissioner did accept the bail money and allowed me to go home for eight days. As I gathered my things and was ready to leave, my lawyer asked if I had enough for bus fare. Even though I had money hidden in my clothes, I told him I had none, so he gave me five rupees for the trip.

When I arrived home, my small daughters were overjoyed to see me again. My younger one would not let me out of her sight. It was even difficult for me to have privacy to go to the bathroom!

During those few days I was home, a police officer on a tour in the area visited my home and verified for the commissioner that indeed my children had no mother and that my mother-in-law did live with us. His report satisfied the authorities, even though they previously had doubted my claim to be the only one to support my family.

Eight days later I returned for the trial. As I started to leave, my younger daughter clung to me and cried for me to take her. You should have seen the judge's face when she appeared with me. "Why did you bring her?"

"Your honor, she would not let me out of her sight all the time I was home! She begged me not to leave her, so what could I to do?"

The jailer piped up, "What will we do with her?"

"She will stay with me in jail," I answered. "My family will send food and whatever is needed."

But something better happened. First, Willie had returned from India and talked with the judge regarding my case. Second, their own policeman had verified my statement that I was the only breadwinner for my family. With these two factors in my favor, the judge released me. I was free to return home.

✝

Not long after my first wife's death my family started thinking about another wife for me. My maternal aunt wanted me to marry one of her daughters, but that idea didn't appeal to me. Another option surfaced, however, which was more to my liking—my maternal cousin, Zubeda.

Marrying cousins is a common practice in my country. There are several advantages of such an arrangement:

1. It keeps the inheritance within the family.

2. It makes it easier for the family to accept a new daughter-in-law, because they have known her from childhood.

3. It provides built-in help, especially in raising children. In some situations, in-laws, aunts, uncles, and grandparents live together as an extended family, with each family unit having its own living quarter but sharing the courtyard and kitchen.

4. It provides security as required by culture for young girls and women when they go outside their home.

When the wedding occurred, our families got two "performances" for the price of one. It was a double wedding. On the day Zubeda and I were married, Zubeda's brother married my sister.

Because I had two daughters by my first wife, and my sister had two sons by her first husband, my mother thought it best that the two sets of children marry each other when they became of age. I didn't go for that at all. This set off sparks, which caused my mother and sister to cut off relations with Zubeda. Even Zubeda's brother would not visit our house. This pleased me to no end, since he and I had never been friends.

My only regret with the estranged relationships was that it pained Zubeda, because she loved her brother and missed him very much. For a special religious holiday she even asked her father to tell her brother to visit us. I did not know of the invitation, but wondered why she had prepared extra food for the festive meal. Her brother was happy to think we might patch things up, but there was a hindrance—my explosive nature.

A few months back I had opened a candy shop in a room attached to our house. One day I was in the shop when I heard the voice of Zubeda's brother. His unexpected arrival greatly upset me, so I stormed out of the sweet shop and yelled, "What are you doing here?"

As my face reddened and my temple veins bulged, I picked up a stone and ordered my brother-in-law to stay out of the house. He complied, but soon after he left, I heard Zubeda weeping bitterly.

I angrily questioned, "What's the matter with you? Are you upset just because I refused to let that useless brother of yours enter our house?" Without waiting for an answer, I angrily poured the chicken curry and rice onto the dirt floor, stomped my foot in it, and threw pieces of meat against the wall! Then I retreated back to the sweet shop in a huff.

I was awakened that night by Zubeda's crying. "All the other children had new clothes today," she sobbed. "They ate meals together and were happy, but our children had none of that. They're confused. I want them to be happy like other children. Don't you care that our children are suffering from this?"

At first her tears and pleading had little effect, but gradually my bitter attitude softened. I realized the effects of my outburst on the family and changed my mind, so I told Zubeda to get up and prepare another meal. At the same time I went to my candy shop next door and prepared special sweets for the children. At last, around midnight, we were able to have a celebration for the special holiday—somber, but special.

NEW COUNTRY AND NEW RESPONSIBILITY

Most people go through exhausting moves of family and furnishing when settling into a new country. I didn't have to move an inch. The new country came to me.

On August 14, 1947, Pakistan became a new nation and proudly unfurled its green and white flag. For years, Muslims in India were subject to the British and often worked under Hindus. The British ruled but gave most positions of leadership to Hindus. Most Muslims wanted to be free from the Hindu overlords and have their own government.

When the British drew up boundaries for the new country, they took into account that most Muslims were concentrated in the eastern and western areas of India. Pakistan, therefore, became a country with two parts, separated by one thousand miles of India. These Muslim portions were known as West Pakistan, which became Pakistan, and East Pakistan, which later became Bangladesh.

Lord Mountbatten had the task of overseeing the partition of India into two countries. It was a turbulent time in which hundreds of thousands of Hindus and Muslims were killed, as both groups attempted to reach their destinations—Muslims surging to the east and west borders of India and Hindus massing toward India.

After the dust settled, Muslims began to take over deserted Hindu businesses and buildings. This resettlement directly affected me in a way no one could have imagined. A friend of mine was rummaging through a deserted Hindu's house and found a book written by a Hindu. He gave the book to me and casually said that he had no need for it. (The truth of the matter was that he could not read.)

I took the book and eagerly began to read the Hindu's critical observations of the Bible. Wow! This was just what I had been looking for. It reinforced all that I had heard about Christians changing the Bible. However, as I read on, I had to backpedal, for I came to a section in which the author also criticized the Holy Quran. I had never heard anything negative about the Quran in my whole life. I didn't know how to respond to negative criticism about the book so dear to my heart. Anger welled up in my heart.

This Hindu author quoted Sura 2:6 as an example of the lack of logic in the Quran.

> As to those who reject faith, it is the same to them whether you warn them or do not warn them; they will not believe.

My response was, "What kind of God is this?" I had never seen this verse as a problem, but now it was. Even though it was in the Quran, it didn't make sense. The only time the thought of an unjust God had ever so slightly entered my mind was the baffling statement in the New Testament, which I had read at Willie Sutherland's house.

> He has blinded their eyes, and he hardened their heart; lest they see with their eyes, and perceive with their heart, and be converted, and I heal them.
>
> John 12:40

Was this one of the areas Christians had changed? Was it possible the Quran was saying the same confusing thing? I was baffled!

As I contemplated its meaning, this statement seemed to say, "If God planned beforehand that a person could never become a believer, that person has no choice in the matter and is doomed without any hope whatsoever. Why? God has already put a seal on his ears and heart and a cover over his eyes. That could not be the fault of the doomed person. Would God punish that person, even though he is unable to respond? That is unfair."

Again I was left with the question. "What kind of God is this? Why did he send prophets with such a confusing message?"

An illustration popped into my mind. "No father would send his son to get something that the father knew very well was not there and then punish him for not bringing it. If God himself seals hearts and ears and blinds eyes to spiritual teaching so they cannot obey him, then why should he punish those already caught up in his eternal decision? That kind of God certainly was not for me."

"Suppose," I thought, "my master takes me to a barn and shows me a water buffalo. He also shows me food and water for the buffalo and a bucket to use when milking the buffalo. He tells me my work is to feed and water the buffalo, wash it in a nearby canal, and milk it at the end of the day. He adds, 'If you do this work well, you will be rewarded in the evening. If not, you will be punished severely.' After instructing me, he takes me inside his house and locks me in.

"In the evening the master comes, unlocks the door, and asks if I have fed and watered the buffalo and milked her. What could my answer be? My response would have to be, 'I have done nothing you ordered.' Upon hearing my answer the master burns with anger and takes out his sword to kill me.

"Why? Would it be my fault? Or is it the fault of the master? He was the one who locked me inside. How could I possibly obey his commands? I would be innocent. In spite of that he punishes me. This seems to be the situation in which we find ourselves before God, since God is the one who blinds eyes and closes ears, so a man cannot receive and understand his message. Yet he keeps telling me to do things beyond my ability! What a strange and unfair God!"

I was desperate for answers. For four and a half years, I asked every *imam* I met, "Is there really a God? Is there really a day of judgment? Is there really a heaven or hell? Could it be that all the so-called revelations and dreams and visions are nothing but a figment of man's imagination? Is there really a book from heaven? Are angels real? Has anyone seen God? Has he really appointed some men to be prophets or messengers?

"What happens when religious leaders advise people how to live? People can object that these leaders also are mere humans and have no authority to tell others what to do. The only difference is that they claim that God told them what to say. What proof do they have?"

My questions continued: "How did religion begin? How did holy books reach us? Are there paper mills in heaven? Are there printing presses in heaven? Does mail come to earth from heaven?" These thoughts passed furiously through my mind.

God knew what he was doing, as he was stirring up my inquiring mind, but I was not aware of his plans for me.

Because of my doubts and questions, my relatives, friends, and religious leaders tried to pound some sense into my head. They wanted me to become a strong Muslim like my father. Neither my father nor any other *imam* I knew ever questioned anything in the Quran. They wondered why I was different. When I didn't respond the way they thought I should, they concluded I was mentally unbalanced.

About this time, my father was called to a village to speak at the annual celebration of the birth of the prophet Mohammed, but I refused to go. A few days later, several men from our village went to the celebration. As soon as they arrived, my father asked for news from home.

"How's my son doing?"

What he heard was a great disappointment.

"He's a weirdo. He hasn't said his prayers since you left. Furthermore, he openly denies all our religion's teachings. He says he doesn't believe in God, in our prophet, in God's messengers, in his angels, in the judgment, in punishment and rewards, or even in the holy books. We're at our wits end and don't know how long we can put up with him in the village." This report was very upsetting for my father and seemed to sap his physical and mental strength.

A few days later the meetings ended, and my father and his followers started the trip back home. On the way my father became so weak he could not walk. The men accompanying him borrowed a rope bed from a neighboring village and carried him the rest of the way. Once they got him home, he grew weaker and weaker. All attempts of treatment were of no avail. He died two days later.

As news of his death spread, people came from the surrounding areas to mourn his passing. A very influential man, Mr. Sahibzada, was among the mourners. Immediately upon arriving, he took me aside. From our conversation he made a decision. In front of the assembly he requested me to take over the position and responsibilities of my father. I was hesitant to accept, but even Zubeda agreed that I was the only one capable of those responsibilities.

At the insistence of everyone in the village, I relented and accepted the position. I also agreed to go to a well-known local *imam* with much experience and wisdom. There I would receive the necessary training. Although I already knew a lot of what he taught, I did learn more about Islamic law, rituals, teacher-disciple relationships, religious instructions, making of amulets (small charms worn around the neck containing verses from the Quran), and methods of prayer. At that time I was in the mood for the training. I was in the process of reading through the entire Quran, as required for family during the forty days immediately following the death of a family member.

After I completed the training, J'haan Shah placed a colorful headpiece on me to indicate my position as the new *imam* in our village. This J'haan Shah had been the spiritual teacher of my father years ago and now had the privilege of presenting me to my father's followers as his replacement.

When I appeared wearing the headpiece, a strange thing happened. Those who saw me thought for sure that my father had returned. In fact, everyone thought I looked exactly like my father.

Some exclaimed, "News of his father's death must have been a mistake." One elderly woman began to weep bitterly and lashed out at people who had told her that my father was dead. In her mind my father was standing right there in front of her. However,

J'haan Shah assured her and the others, "His father did die. You must accept this fact. However, you are very fortunate. This is his son, made in his mold and very capable of leading you."

What a strange situation! Here I was, a person who for some time completely denied God, denied our prophet, and did not accept the holy books. Now I was forced to pretend to be their spiritual leader. I played the part well. In front of them I seemed to become lost in divine meditation and appeared to be a genuine worshipper of God. I gave the impression of being an expert in religious matters. Elders and faithful followers throughout the area flocked to me day and night and talked endlessly about my dedicated life and abilities as a religious instructor.

My father had been a man of great knowledge and spent much time in holy meditation. He was a very serious student of Islam, but was not very personable. I, on the other hand, had charisma. I was clever and sometimes devious in dealing with my followers. I sometimes told them incidents from the Bible, from what little I had read of the stories of Moses, David, and Jesus—but they had no inkling about the source of these stories.

My simple followers did not realize that I was only pretending to be a strong Muslim. I was totally different on the inside. Since they could not see through my hypocrisy, they proudly exclaimed:

"Glory to God. The son is such a great scholar, a teller of truth, and a worshipper of the Almighty God." As the effect of my charisma increased, people became increasingly enraptured with me—but it began to wear.

All this acting could not continue forever. Pretending to be such a spiritual leader wore me down. People constantly asked boring questions, questions they should have been able to answer themselves. Why couldn't they go to someone else for advice?

One day, without consulting anyone, I simply quit. I had had enough. I gave the financial account for building the mosque to J'haan Shah and then turned my back on the whole endeavor.

It was left to J'haan Shah to inform my followers that I had returned to Pind Sultani and would no longer be their spiritual leader. It took a while for the sudden change to sink into the minds of those who had been living on a spiritual high from the time I had become their leader. Their enthusiasm and expectations soon vanished, when it hit home that they no longer had a leader.

THE BATTLE OF THE BOOKS

Back in Pind Sultani, I quickly slipped back into my old ways. I left the life of religious teaching as if it had never happened. I was involved again in old habits and devilish activities. To help make ends meet, I re-opened a candy shop next door to our house, but my mind remained filled with agnostic ideas and doubts.

One day I found something interesting. Near my house was a pond. It usually was filled with water, but due to a lack of rain it had dried up and developed large cracks. In the cracks I noticed innumerable colorful worms about the size of grains of rice.

Sometime they bunched together, and sometimes they separated and crawled away from each other. This greatly amazed me.

As I was looking at it, the leader of the local mosque came by. I said to him in a lighthearted manner, "Imam Sahib, come and see what is in this dried up pond." He paid no attention, so I took some of the worms for him to see. In disgust, he finally looked to see what I had in my hand, so I pointed to the worms and asked, "What are these things?"

The *imam* responded in great anger, "These worms are your father," comparing me to a worm.

I then asked, "How did they come into being?"

"God made them."

I then asked, "If I were to mix some things together and from that mixture make worms like this, would you also call me God?"

The *imam* could stand no more of such nonsense and walked away, calling me a foul-mouthed ignoramus. After evening prayers, he announced to everyone in the mosque, "Beware of Qureshi. He is very arrogant and no longer has control of his senses. Who knows? At any time he might announce that he himself is God. He's completely out of his mind."

He then spoke very directly to one of my close friends and ordered him not to keep company with me anymore.

"This son of our honorable Shah Sahib has gone completely mad. If you keep hanging around him, he will draw you away from Islam. If you continue being his friend, Allah will *not* answer your prayers.

"Let me put it this way. You have a choice: either completely cut yourself off from him, or quit coming to the mosque for prayers. He is a renegade and has completely turned against our religion. It is imperative that none of us have any dealings with him." My friend stood in silence and then slowly walked away without a response. But he was so concerned for me that, in spite of the strict warning, he knew he had to contact me.

The following morning I was on my way to the market to get whole-wheat flour. My friend called out to me. I parked my bicycle and went into his shop. He ushered me into a back room and asked me to sit down.

"There is something I have to tell you in private. Right now we are alone, just the two of us—plus God."

I interrupted, "You're partially correct. I am here and you are here, but where is God?"

My friend started to explain, "God is that being who created all things. He is present every place all the time. He is always present. This means he also is here."

I retorted, "Those are only thoughts of your imagination." With that I removed my turban and said, "If God is here, then tell him to bring some pieces of candy that are lying in my house and put them here. If he does, I will believe there is a God and that he is present with us."

My friend looked at me for some time but remained silent. Then he gently took the turban from my hand, put it back on my head and led me outside. We sat down in front of his shop, and he gave me the customary cup of tea.

"I am telling you exactly as it is. Yesterday you said some things to Imam Sahib that prompted him to declare to all of us that we are not to have anything to do with you. He pointed me out in particular and insisted that I stop having any association with you or else—"

"Or else, what?" I interrupted.

"Or else stop coming to the mosque for daily prayers. He doesn't want any of us to associate with a person who denies God, the day of judgment, and the prophets. He said that anyone who has anything to do with you alienates himself from God. He added that God will not accept the prayers of anyone who associate with you.

"Now tell me—how can I, as a devout Muslim, stop my daily prayers? You and I have been close friends for thirty years, so please heed my advice. In that way 'the snake will be killed, and the stick will not be broken.'" (This is, in our Urdu language, similar to "You can't have your cake and eat it, too.")

By this time I was listening intently to my friend, and he continued.

"If you read an Urdu translation of the Quran, you will understand it better. In this way you will come to know God. You will find the purpose for which you were born."

I lowered my head and humbly replied, "Since you are my true and trusted friend and have a genuine concern for me, I will do as you say. But you know what? Over the past four years I have asked every *imam* I met, 'Where is God? If there is one, what kind of God is he?' They all thought I was losing my mind, but not one of them was able to give me a satisfactory answer."

After I agreed to his advice, we parted ways. I went home and thought, *I cannot possibly talk with God. I'm only human, but God is far beyond the reach of a mere man.* Nevertheless, I took the Quran, which I doubted, and went into the house. For a long time I sat thinking and wondering how I could believe in the Quran, knowing that there is no God who could have written it.

Finally, I broke down and cried out: "If you really are God, and this book really is your word, and the prophet Mohammed is your prophet, and you really gave this book, then please forgive me for being misled by Satan. Lead me so I can understand your word and be able to follow it. I will have you as my true master and follow Mohammed as your divinely appointed prophet. I really want to believe in you and follow your teachings in the Holy Quran." As I became aware of God, I had comfort and peace. My thoughts changed to adoration and I called out: "Praise God! His ways are wonderful!"

What a change! For four years I had been an infidel and openly denied that God existed. Suddenly I had become a genuine Muslim, a faithful follower of Islam and no longer a hypocrite. There was just one nagging question, however, that continued to hound me. It was the book written by a Hindu, who criticized both Islam and Christianity. The Hindu pointed out that God of Islam requires so much from his followers, but does not give the ability to obey. Such a God would be unjust. I finally decided to put this out of my mind for the time being.

I did find, however, that when I read the Quran in my own language, I understood it much more clearly than reading it in Arabic. I was surprised to learn that the Quran called God the God of all creatures. This was a new insight, for I had always heard that heaven was only for Muslims.

I became more alert when I saw that the Quran states that true believers are those who are faithful in prayers, help the poor, say the creed, believe in the day of judgment, and believe in the four books God had sent through His prophets: Moses, David, Jesus, and Mohammed. I noticed that the first three of the four are included in the Christians' holy book. I read, for example, in Sura 5:44, 46, 48:

> It was we who revealed the law to Moses; therein was guidance and light. By its standard have been judged the Jews, by the prophets who bowed to Allah's will, by the rabbis and the doctors of law. For to them we entrusted the protection of Allah's book, and they were witnesses thereto: therefore fear not men, but fear me, and do not sell my signs for a miserable price. If any do fail to judge by what Allah has revealed, they are unbelievers ... And in their footsteps we sent Jesus the son of Mary, confirming the law that had come before him; we sent him the Gospel; therein was guidance and light, and confirmation of the law that had come before him; a guidance and an admonition to those who fear Allah ... To you we sent the Scripture in truth, *confirming the scripture that came before it, and guarding it in safety ...*

I paused and thought about these words, "...guarding it in safety." Did this mean God had preserved even the Christians' book from change? I determined to get to the bottom of that very important question.

In Sura 5:68, I found the following verse to be a challenge:

> Say, oh people of the book, you have no ground to stand upon unless you stand fast by the Law, the Gospel, and all the revelation that has come to you from your Lord.

When I read this, I realized that Jews, Christians, and Muslims all are people of the Book. I concluded that the books of Moses, of David, of Jesus, and the Quran comprise one set of rules God has for all men. I couldn't shake the daunting question, "Is it possible that I can accept the Christians' book with as much confidence as I accept the Quran?"

I realized that I was obligated to follow what God had revealed in the Quran. As a result of the promise I made to read the Quran in Urdu, I found myself being pulled along in a stream of questions I had never before encountered. I realized that if I didn't read the book of Moses, the Psalms, and the Injeel, I would be unfaithful to the prophets. The Quran and the Injeel were becoming more fascinating and helpful than ever before. (*Injeel* is Arabic for the New Testament. Muslims understand it as "the book of Jesus.")

As I read about the miracles of Jesus, I saw them from a new viewpoint. How could Jesus raise the dead? How was he able to make the blind to see or the lame to walk? How was all this possible? Only God could do such miracles.

Sura 3:45–49 also helped me, for it tells of the virgin birth of Jesus Christ and some of his miracles:

> The angel said to Miriam [Mary], God gives you good news about one called Jesus Christ the son of Miriam, who is very close to God and who will have a high position in the last days of the world and in the world to come.
>
> Miriam asked the angel, 'How is this possible, since no man has ever touched me?'
>
> The angel replied that whatever God commands to come into existence, that thing comes into existence. God will make Jesus a messenger from Israel. He will tell people that he had come from God and use signs to prove it. He would make a bird from the dirt, blow into it the breath of life, and it would become a living creature. He would give sight to those born blind, heal lepers and the lame, cast out evil spirits and heal the sick. He would cause the dead to come out of their graves. He also would tell a person what he had eaten and what he had in his house.

I was now ready to believe that God really did give inspiration to prophets by means of dreams and visions. I also realized that no one knows the future except Almighty God. The prophet Mohammed could not predict the future, even though Muslims believe him to be the greatest of all prophets. Yet in the Injeel, Jesus Christ often spoke of future events, some of which were fulfilled within a few decades of his death. For example, in Luke 21:6, Jesus tells about the destruction of Jerusalem in 70 AD.

I now understood that only Jesus could foretell things that God alone knows. Suddenly, my attitude towards Jesus, the son of Mary, changed! If I had not read it in the Quran, I would never have believed it.

I now read Isaiah 7:14 with new understanding. "Behold, the virgin shall conceive and bear a son …" Previously it was meaningless for me, but with my new understanding, the virgin birth of Jesus fits the description of Sura 3:47, where Mary says, "Oh my Lord, how shall I have a son, when no man has touched me?" Sura 19:20–21 gives the same words of Mary.

> How shall I have a son, seeing that no man has touched me, and I am not unchaste? But the Lord said, 'It is easy for me. It is a matter decreed from eternity.'"

I began to see how the pieces fit together. I found it fascinating to compare God's creation of man in the Garden of Eden with a miracle of Christ recorded in the Quran. In the Bible, God formed a man's body out of dirt. When he breathed into that form, it became a living being (Gen. 2:7). Then the Quran says, in Sura 5:110, that Jesus made a bird out of dirt, breathed life into it, and it flew away. In other words Jesus did the very work of creation as ascribed to God. Gradually, the Quran was paving the way for me to understand who Jesus Christ really is. It now made sense. He who does what only God can do—must be God!

The mention of Jesus in the Quran so roused my interest that I began to read the Gospels to gain more insight into his birth, life, suffering, death, and resurrection. The story of Jesus's death and resurrection shook me, for the Quran denies both of these events. I realized that both holy books could not be true. One says he died on the cross and three days later came to life again; the other, that he did not die on the cross. Islam teaches that he somehow was taken alive from the cross and transported directly into heaven. Which one should I believe?

Since both books speak of the virgin birth of Jesus, I concentrated on his birth. The more I thought about it, the more I realized its uniqueness. From that time a new thought hit me; there are four different kinds of birth found in the Bible:

1. God's creation of Adam and Eve
2. Natural birth as the result of parents having a child
3. Christ's virgin birth
4. Spiritual birth through belief in the death and resurrection of the Lord Jesus.

This was not only entirely new for me, it was more wonderful than anything I had ever heard before, for it meant that I could be ready for heaven.

MY DILEMMA: TO TELL OR NOT TO TELL

By 1958, I had confessed my sins to the Lord, but I had trouble deciding whether to let it be known or not. To help with this weighty problem I checked with friends better acquainted with the Bible than I. Their input, plus the Holy Spirit working in my life, made it was obvious what I was to do. I would begin to talk about the one who changed my life. My changed life had already spoken louder than any words I used during the days of my early walk with Jesus, but I realized I needed to describe with words how it happened. To this end, I began memorizing verses from the Bible.

It was not easy when I began to tell other people what Jesus had done for me. Of course I told only Muslims, because I assumed that all Christians had experienced salvation. As I began to tell others about Jesus Christ, I gained more confidence with each experience. I was so thankful for the encouraging words of Jesus in Matthew 10:19, "…do not worry about what to say or how to say it. At that time you will be given what to say."

My explaining God's plan of salvation also helped Zubeda have a foundation for what God soon would do in her life. Up to this time, she had only seen the changes in my life. Now she was hearing and understanding the reason for those changes.

Zubeda overheard me tell different ones about the work Jesus had done in my life. She knew that before I started to read the Injeel I could explode in anger at the drop of a hat. But as I read that wonderful book, she noticed a remarkable transformation. My treatment of her and the children changed dramatically. Due to the changes in me, she began reading the Bible for herself and was also captivated by its teachings. She even understood its teachings better than she could understand the teachings of the Quran. The message of the Bible began working like a magnet, drawing her to it. She loved its message of love and concern, which was a great contrast with parts of the Quran that teach revenge and hatred. But the biggest factor in her sudden interest in the Injeel was the undeniable and unbelievable change she saw me. Whatever it was about that book, she was hungry to know.

As the message of the New Testament began to penetrate her life, her brothers became increasingly upset. They bombarded her with objections and questions to make her change her mind.

"What are you doing? You'll be separated from your father and brothers. Your children will suffer for this. Why cause all this trouble for yourself and your family?"

She didn't budge! I was beginning to learn the value of a faithful wife. "Her worth is far above jewels" (Proverbs 31:10).

The Lord worked in many ways to soften and mold me into the kind of husband he wanted me to be. In our culture, the role of a wife often is not the most pleasant—and this is true both in Muslim and "Christian" families in Pakistan. Zubeda proved to be a faithful wife in spite of many heartaches brought on by my old self. Many times she could have left me because of my outbursts of anger and animosity toward her and her family. But she remained true!

Fortunately, I emerged as a new person when I found Jesus Christ as my Savior and Lord. I did not change religions. I merely left a system of trying to obey God and get to heaven by my own efforts (a simple definition of any religion) and accepted Jesus Christ who said, "I have come that they might have life" (John 10:10).

Zubeda much preferred my new life in Christ above good relations with her own blood relatives. They showed none of the love and concern she knew Jesus had given me. I could give innumerable examples of such changes, but here is one for which I am so thankful.

For some time my wife and I lived in Fatah Jung, in my mother's house instead of being in our own house in Pind Sultani. One day Zubeda visited her parents in Pind Sultani, where I had locked our house to safeguard the household items. I had given the key to Zubeda's cousin, Bashir, and asked him to take valuable items out of the house and store them in his own house for safekeeping.

Instead of putting our things in his own home, however, he sold our household items to various families in the village and pocketed the money. Neither Bashir's parents nor Zubeda knew anything of his deceitful act. To make matters worse, the money he got from selling our furnishings he gambled away— and lost everything.

When I arrived in Pind Sultani to be with Zubeda, Bashir quickly gave the key to Zubeda's father and ran away. I was unaware of all this but had a questioning thought when I discovered that Zubeda's father had the key. I took the key and went to check things at our house.

All I found were empty boxes scattered everywhere. I immediately thought this was the work of my in-laws, so I darted off to their house to demand a reason for their action. The encounter ended in double accusations. I thought my in-laws were guilty, and they assumed I was trying to stir up trouble. Both sides were puzzled, so we all went together to see what had happened. Zubeda burst into tears as she saw our empty rooms.

Finally, someone realized that Bashir was nowhere in sight. We asked around and learned that he had sold our things right there in the village. We also heard two days later that there was a theft at the police station. Bashir turned out to be the culprit for that theft also. At that point the police went into action.

When they found Bashir, they beat him, handcuffed him, and brought him to the station. They were ready to put him behind bars, but Bashir's parents were so crushed at the dishonor for the family of having a son in jail that they offered to pay for everything Bashir had stolen. Because of their willingness to care for the loss, I dropped the charges. After that the relationship with my father-in-law improved a bit—but only for a brief spell.

Before long something happened and my father-in-law again became very angry with me. No one knows why, but when I sat down for a meal, he exploded in anger. Before I could eat anything, he grabbed my plate and told me to get out of the house.

I was boiling mad, and I quickly returned home. Unfortunately, I vented my feelings on Zubeda. But bless her heart—in spite of my unreasonable treatment of her, she refused to lash back at me. She remained a faithful and obedient wife. Some time later I found, in Proverbs 18:22, a description that so beautifully described my admiration for Zubeda: "He who finds a wife finds a good thing."

Further Confirmation

Let me back up a little with my story. When I was seriously considering whether to let it be known that I had become a Christian, I went to the local holy man, who was a personal friend and highly respected in our community. Holy men are different from *imams*. Imams led daily prayers. Holy men were supposedly more in direct contact with God and the spirit world than *imams* and, therefore, had access to information not afforded others. I was certain he would provide the guidance I needed. Before reaching his house I was emotionally overwhelmed with the way things were going and sat down near the village well to collect my thoughts. While sitting in solitude tears came to my eyes.

At that time of day, colorfully clad women were coming to fill water jars. One of them saw me crying and asked, "What's the matter? Why are you crying?" I gave a lame excuse and sauntered towards the holy man's house. A number of people were already waiting for their turn to hear his words of wisdom. The questions and confessions were not private, since everyone in line could hear the problems of those farther ahead.

One complaint I overheard was by a man whose brothers had spread rumors about him and then fired him from the job he had with them. With tears in his eyes, he implored the holy man, "How could brothers do this to their own kin?"

The holy man fumbled with his prayer beads and slowly shook his head.

"Try not let it bother you. Look for another job, and keep your chin up. It's the will of Allah."

The man with this problem was one of my long-time friends. I was greatly disappointed to see him leave more perplexed than when he came. He had drawn a blank. My dejected friend turned and walked slowly away.

Nevertheless, I stayed in line, hoping the holy man would have good advice for me. I also wanted to tell the holy man about my interest in Christianity and that I had found the Bible and its teaching so different from Islamic teaching that I wanted to learn more about that book. As these thoughts were in my mind, my crestfallen friend strolled over and stood nearby.

With tears in his eyes, he turned towards me and said, "Brother Qureshi, Christians are not like this. They learn to love their enemies, but in our religion even a brother turns against his brother. Their religion must be better than ours." He had no idea how pertinent and powerful his words were for me just at that particular moment.

When I heard his comment, the thought hit me, *I no longer need advice from the holy man.* My friend's incisive comment had clearly answered my questions. I left my place in the queue and started home, feeling assured that the teachings of the Injeel are correct and that I was ready to let it be known that I had become a follower of Jesus Christ. I walked into our house with a heart full of joy and peace. I was becoming a "new creature in Christ" (2 Cor. 5:17).

Soon the Lord gave me another seal of approval for my decision. The very next day my daughter, Aqeela, was playing near a fig tree when a water buffalo gouged her arm with its horn. The force of its horn tore out a piece of flesh, but very little blood oozed from the injury. Zubeda took her to a doctor, who was amazed as he saw the open gap in her bicep and heard the story. Why so little blood? News of this nearly bloodless wound spread quickly, and people flocked to see her arm. Our Muslim friends shouted praises to Allah, for they considered it a sign of divine blessing on our family.

I was on my way home when the doctor met me on the path and explained what had happened. Through it all, Aqeela felt very little pain, even though it looked as if someone had scooped a spoonful of flesh from her arm.

It had its effect on me, too. I took it as another sign from the Lord that I had made the right decision. I had a strong sense of confirmation that I was on the right track, and it felt good.

Later I learned God had even more in store for me. There was another incident of God's special protection for my family. Our son, Shafeeq, took wheat to the mill. I had warned him to be very careful when pouring wheat into the grinder, because our loose Pakistani clothing could easily be caught in the machine. There were examples in our own village of this happening. On one occasion a woman's head covering was caught by the machine. She was cruelly killed, as her body was dragged into the crushing jaws of the mill.

Shafeeq was very cautious, for he once had a close call with death at that very mill. While putting grain into the hopper, his pant leg caught in the machinery and was torn to shreds.

"*But God…*"

The machine stopped, and Shafeeq's life was spared.

THE POINT OF NO RETURN

As I started to proclaim myself a Christian, my Muslim relatives and friends responded with little concern.

"You had no religion before, and you have none now. You denied there is a God before; so what is special about your following some pointless idea at this time? However, in spite of your vacillations, you must remember that Islam is the true religion. If you do not believe in the one true God and his prophet Mohammed, you will be condemned to hell forever."

This thought jumped into my mind, even though I remained silent: "I wish you could realize the assurance I have of going to heaven (1 John 5:13). I know that not one of you can say that."

If I were to have asked any of them, "Are you going to heaven?" my Muslim friends would have only one answer. "No one can know that until judgment day. Then, and only then, will God reveal who gets to heaven and who will not. It's his decision, and he doesn't tell anyone until that time."

Qureshi family learning God's Word

The unending pressure for me to return to Islam was a blessing in disguise. It was hard to hear their harsh and angry words and to see the hatred in their faces, but their scorn forced me to depend on the Lord Jesus. With greater reliance on the Lord, it became easier to tell people that I had become a follower of Jesus Christ. However, I suddenly realized that I had to face a problem harder to overcome than the insults and persuasions from my relatives and friends. How would I tell my wife? Would she be willing to continue living with me? Would she want to leave and return to her parent's home? I wanted so badly for her to stay with me, but the decision would be hers.

After an evening meal, I tried to work up the courage to explain my decision to her. With sweaty hands and a rapidly beating heart, I explained my total commitment to Jesus Christ.

"Zubeda, we have had a wonderful life together. God has given us these precious children, but Zubeda, I have found something even more important than an earthly family. I have found forgiveness for all my filthy sins that you know so well. Jesus Christ has also given me a brand new spiritual life full of love, joy, and peace. This means I am now a Christian. I want so badly for you to join me in this new life and joy, but I cannot force you. If you prefer, you can leave and continue living as a Muslim with your father and siblings. Or—you can stay with me and learn with me the ways of the Injeel."

A smile of relief and joy broke out on my face as she grabbed my arm and said, "Qureshi, my beloved, I love you and will gladly stay. I've never seen such a change in anyone, and I want what you have." Tears came to our eyes as we embraced in the privacy of our own home.

Word Spread of My Changed Life

On one occasion, I returned to Fatah Jung and learned that a foreigner had come to the village to meet me. He had heard a rumor that someone in Fatah Jung had become a Christian and wanted to check it out. Fortunately, he had left a note saying he lived in the mission house in Attock City. I learned that it was the very house in which Willie Sutherland had lived. The name of my visitor was Bill Dalton.

In a few days I made my way to the mission house in Attock City and was greeted by Mr. Dalton. I explained how I had become a follower of Jesus Christ and that I finally understood what the Lord Jesus had done for me. My problem, however, was that I knew nothing about the Christian way of life.

"How do Christians pray? Why do they sing so much? What do I have to do when entering a church building? Do I remove my shoes as when entering a mosque? Will I have to wear a head covering as when saying Islamic prayers? What special days do Christians observe? What else do I need to know to live as a Christian?"

As I listened to answers to these questions, one subject grabbed my attention. It was something entirely new for me; something I did not expect. A Christian is one who has been forgiven. He in turn must forgive others. Then I heard something that made me cringe.

"A Christian must also ask for forgiveness, when necessary."

"Ask forgiveness? Now just a minute! Many times I have mistreated my wife. I often became angry and took out my frustration on her. You mean I have to ask forgiveness from her? I can ask forgiveness from many people, but to ask forgiveness from my wife? That would be the most humiliating thing I've ever done. No one does that in my country!" But as this teaching of the Injeel sank in, I realized it was a step I would have to take—if I wanted to obey God's word.

After my missionary brother prayed, I asked for permission to leave and cycled back home. On the way, I tried to figure how to ask my wife for forgiveness, but no words came to mind. On the other hand, to be a follower of Jesus Christ, I would have to overcome this hurdle. As I continued pedaling, I kept asking the Lord to help me do something, which, in my own strength, was impossible.

I reached home and found Zubeda had prepared a meal. During the meal of curried lentils and fresh *chappatis* (flat tortilla-type bread—only better!) I chatted with Zubeda, but in the back of my mind, I knew I'd have to get to the point before long. As I was arguing with myself whether to carry through with this newfound conviction, I felt the Spirit of the Lord empower me.

I humbly stood before my wife with tears in my eyes.

"Zubeda, I have mistreated you many times. I remember the time I kicked your brother out of our house. I remember the special holiday when our children had no new clothes, nor special food and sweets. I remember when I would not allow you to visit your parents. When I learned that you secretly met with your mother near a graveyard, I swore at you—even though it was no fault of yours. I remember throwing away the delicious meal you had prepared for a special holiday and that I angrily stomped on the pieces of meat lying on the floor. I remember the time I purposely scared you by locking you in a room and threatening to kill you.

"Zubeda, since I became a follower of Jesus, I have learned things that I never knew before. A missionary brother taught me from the Bible how a husband should treat his wife. He told me things about forgiveness I had never heard. I learned that not only should I forgive others, but that when I have done wrong, I am to ask forgiveness. In reality, you are a wonderful wife and you are very precious to me. Will you forgive me for all the wrong I did against you?"

Zubeda didn't know how to react to my unexpected behavior. This was a different man than she had been married to for several years—but she was overjoyed by the change!

From the time I began to read the Bible openly, she had clearly seen the difference in the way I now treated her and others. I was entirely different from what I had been before. She had had no idea what I was learning from the Bible, but it aroused her interest in that forbidden book. When I took the difficult step of asking forgiveness from her, she was all the more determined to learn about Jesus and about forgiveness of her sins, too. She desperately wanted the same kind of life I had so recently found. What a joy that we were now not only "one flesh" as man and wife, now we were also one spirit in the Lord Jesus Christ.

Her relatives, however, did not share her excitement. A few days later she had to make a visit to her parents. In most countries the death of an animal does not cause much of a ripple in a family. In developing countries like Pakistan, however, certain animals are a necessity. Families pay large sums to have a milk-producing water buffalo. When one dies, it is a great financial loss. So when Zubeda heard that her father's water buffalo had died, a visit to mourn the loss of the animal was mandatory.

I told her to take one of our daughters and visit her father. She was glad for my permission, as it had been years since I had allowed her to visit him. Her father was glad to see her, but was concerned about her interest in Christianity and tried to stop her from reading the Bible. She responded to his concern by reviewing again the tremendous change in my life.

"Qureshi actually asked forgiveness for his unfair treatment of me. Something wonderful has happened in his life that I have never seen in anyone before. This is the result of his reading the Bible. Why should I stop reading a book that is so powerful? The Bible teaches that I have a Father in heaven who will care for me and that Jesus Christ gave his life for me by shedding his blood on the cross."

At that, her brother told her to get out of the house, because she had insulted their father. She left in tears and slowly made her way home. What a relief to get home to a caring husband! Fortunately, she realized that her own faith was being strengthened by that unpleasant experience. She was learning what it means to belong to a heavenly Father who would never throw her out of his presence. What unspeakable joy!

Further Steps of Witnessing

As Zubeda was beginning to take baby steps in her newfound faith, I also was growing in my spiritual life. The more I grew in Christ Jesus, the more I enjoyed talking about Jesus. I knew that my Muslim friends needed to hear what Jesus had done for them, but I had never imagined that so-called Christians also needed to hear the story of salvation by grace alone, apart from works. I had always assumed that every Christian had the same life and joy that Jesus gave me.

I had not been around those in the Christian community very long before I realized that many of them were just as lost as Muslims. Many thought of themselves as Christians simply because they were born in a Christian home. I knew that being born in a Muslim home is how I became a Muslim. Because my parents were Muslims, I was a Muslim! After I learned the difference between being born physically and being born spiritually, I gladly explained the good news of Jesus to "Christians" as well as to Muslims.

I now explained forgiveness of sins through the sacrifice of Christ in our place whether talking to Muslims or to Christians. As a starting point when talking to Muslims, I used the Quran to point out things about Jesus that they are not aware of. When talking to so-called Christians, I used only the Bible.

Since Muslims do not read the Bible, I wrote a small pamphlet that points to Jesus in the Quran. It is entitled *Masee kee shan; uz ruhay Quran* [in Urdu *shahn* and *Qurahn* rhyme], which means, *The Glory of Christ as Revealed in the Quran.* Since teachings from the Quran helped me understand who Jesus is, it stands to reason that other Muslims could learn about him in the same way. I had these pamphlets printed, for I knew they could go places I couldn't go and be read by people I'd never meet.

I also pondered how to be a more effective witness in our village. I wanted to do something to make it obvious that a Christian lived in our village, so I decided to put up a stone on top of our courtyard wall that all could see.

We found a flat-faced stone that would serve the purpose. It was big enough to be seen but small enough that Shafeeq and I could put it up on the wall by ourselves. I needed his help, for no Muslim would help put it up. On it I wrote two simple words: Christ House.

After we cemented it into place, I asked my son-in-law, a professional calligrapher, to write some Scripture verses on the courtyard wall in the beautiful Persian script. He wrote for all to read:

"Do not fret because of evil men" (Psalm 37:1).

"Trust in the Lord and do good, dwell in the land and enjoy safe pasture" (Psalm 37:3).

"Among the nations there is none like you, O Lord … All the nations you have made will come and worship before you; they will bring glory to your name" (Psalm 86:9–10).

The book of Psalms is one of the four books Muslims accept as inspired; my Muslim neighbors would have no objection to these quotes. Notice, however, what stirred up the hornet's nest of animosity. It was the name of Christ that was on the stone. For them his name literally was a " … stone of stumbling and a rock of offense" (Romans 9:33).

Local religious leaders were furious. They were bent on expelling us from their midst. They could take no more. Earlier they were sure they had seen me deny the existence of God. They knew I had stopped saying my prayers. In their sight I had "gone off my rocker." This, in itself, didn't bother them. However, my announcement that I had become a follower of Jesus Christ pushed their panic button. For a person to turn from Islam to follow Jesus was blasphemy. One way or another they would force me to recant or leave the village. It began the following day when the *imam* announced from the mosque that everyone must boycott us.

"Do not have anything to do with this man or his family. Do not let them get water from the village well! Do not sell them anything from your stores. Do not buy anything from them. Throw stones and manure into their courtyard. Write disgraceful slogans on their courtyard walls and door. Force them to come back to Islam or leave our village."

The villagers gladly heeded the *imam*'s strict orders. When it was time to draw water, local men did not let any member of my family get near the village well. Some of the boys threw manure into our courtyard. The following day, school teachers spent their time instructing their students on writing slogans and banners against us. When they had several banners and insulting notes of protest prepared, the teachers led the students in a march to our house. Some of them had made offensive drawings of me. They berated the Jesus I claimed to follow. Again, it was that name that stirred them up. If only I had not used that name, my troubles would not have happened. This Jesus is called in the Bible the "Son of God," thus making him a partner with God in the mind of Muslims. This is the greatest of all sins, according to Sura 9:30 in the Quran. Their hatred of the name of Jesus describes those mentioned in I Peter 2:8, "A stone of stumbling, and a rock of offense" (ESV).

Our fellow villagers responded to the statements on our courtyard wall by saying they would do one of two things: force us out by *fire* or by *brute force.* One way or another, they would remove us from their midst. Pind Sultani was a Muslim village!

Zubeda was alone with one of our daughters and the grandson we were raising when several *imams* and their followers from the surrounding area were called together to march against our house. I was gone. A crowd soon gathered around the house. They had kerosene and were intent on setting the house on fire.

While the crowd was shouting threats, Zubeda asked Sameena, who was quite young, "Are you ready? They are going to burn us up."

Sameena quickly replied, "I am, for I know we will meet in heaven."

Suddenly from somewhere in the crowd a man's voice boomed out very authoritatively, "*Do not harm this man; he is a good man.*"

No one recognized the voice, but the following day local ladies asked Zubeda, "Who was the man in the crowd around your house? We had never seen him before."

It was then that whispers of an *angel appearance* circulated among the villagers. *Was the Qureshi family divinely protected?* they wondered.

Just because one threat was out of the way did not mean they were content to let the stone stay in such a visible spot. Burning down the house didn't pan out, so they would use force to remove the stone.

The "Christ House" sign on our house proclaimed, "A Christian lives here." It was very offensive for all our neighbors. It was an affront to their religious pride. They decided they could not have a Christian living in their village, especially one who wouldn't be quiet about his religion. Something had to be done!

When one of the villager leaders insisted I remove the stone, I asked him why.

"It pains me and it offends our community." I explained that it took much effort to put it in place and that I did not intend to remove it.

The man shot back, "If that's what you want, here's what you'll get. Tomorrow I will come with four men and we'll take it down." The next day the men came to fulfill that promise.

"But God…"

God again had a different plan. The next day a vendor was selling flavored cold drinks along a well-traveled path near our house. Many men were milling around sipping their drinks and chatting. The man who intended to take down our stone stepped forward and ordered cold drinks for himself and his four helpers. Three other men in the crowd noticed that cold drinks were being handed out, so they pretended to be part of the group. Each took a glass, drank it and departed without paying.

As the man who brought four helpers started to pay the vendor, the vendor also demanded money for the three who left without paying. He assumed they were all in the same group. The leader who ordered the original five glasses was not about to pay for the ones that were taken by false pretense. On the other hand, the vendor was intent on getting his money for all eight. A fight ensued. My accuser and his men overturned the vendor's cart. Drinking glasses fell and broke, ice spilled on the path, and the juice concentrate ran aimlessly toward the open ditch alongside the dirt path. During the melee the vendor's leg was severely injured.

Two policemen soon arrived on foot. They were about to take him to the hospital, but I intervened.

"Not to the hospital. That's too expensive." I made another arrangement for his treatment, which indeed proved cheaper than taking him to the hospital. As a result of my help, the vendor became a very good friend. He had witnessed a Christian life up close. Due to the presence of the policemen, the one whose purpose was to remove the stone decided not to cause trouble. He melted into the crowd and his original plans disintegrated.

At this point I could have gloated over the interruption of the adversary's plan, but God had taught me a better response—love and prayer. This was yet another example of the frequently used biblical phrase, "*But God …*" They determined destruction; *God* determined protection. God was making clear the promise of 1 John 4:4 in my life: "Greater is he who is in you than he who is in the world."

Fellow villagers were ready to use force or fire to cause us to leave the village, but Zubeda's relatives tried persuasion. Her brother again talked with us and earnestly pleaded with us to leave such foolishness.

"Look at all the trouble you are making for yourself and your children. It isn't necessary. All you have to do is renounce this nonsense, and everything will be all right."

Zubeda explained that one day Jesus Christ is coming back to earth, and everyone will have to stand before him.

"You should read the Bible for yourself and see what it says. When he comes back, my husband and I are going to heaven with him. At the Day of Judgment, where will you be? You will be left outside and beat your chest, ruing the day you had a chance to accept him.

"While you still have time, you should accept Jesus Christ. He will forgive you of your sins and you will be ready for heaven. You're a good-looking, young man. You have plenty and live a comfortable life, but one day all that will end."

Again he responded, "You're out of your mind. You're not making any sense."

Her older brother soon arrived and reiterated what the younger brother had said.

Zubeda merely pointed to me and said, "You remember what kind of man he was before he accepted Jesus Christ? He is a changed man. The Bible is a powerful book. Its message has strengthened us and given us peace we had no idea even existed. My husband would never be the man he is now without God having changed his heart. Formerly, there was no peace in our home. We always argued, but that has changed. I have contentment such as I've never known before. Jesus has given me this happiness."

In spite of the trouble from boycotts and opposition of friends and relatives, Zubeda's love for the Lord Jesus prevailed, even when she didn't have much to set before us at meal times. Why? Because of these two small words:

"But God..."

Here's an example. During a boycott, when we could neither buy anything in our village nor get water from the well, local women brought water and supplies to our house at night when their husbands were asleep. Their kindness always bolstered my faith in Jesus and proved to me many times that he always knew exactly what I needed to keep my eyes on him.

FAITH OF THE FAMILY

The Lord gave me six daughters—Naseema, Shameem, Anjaman, Aqeela, Shaheen, and Sameena—but only one son. Since Shafeeq was the only son, he felt a responsibility to protect the family honor. He became visibly nervous when trying to explain what was happening to his father and mother and was apologetic in talking to Muslims about us, even though he personally felt the sting of never-ending complaints about our family.

Zubeda and I often reminded our children that anything we suffered for Jesus was nothing in comparison to what Jesus suffered for us. We purposely tried to talk more about him than about the difficulties he allowed us to face. I had learned that the Bible is a Christ-centered book, and I wanted our personal lives to be Christ-centered, too.

Shafeeq spent much time with his uncle, a leader in the local mosque, and wholeheartedly helped him in his religious duties. The religious leaders he hung around bombarded him with reasons explaining why I had made a big mistake in becoming a Christian. Their reasons and questions propelled Shafeeq into high gear at times to encourage me to back off from following Jesus and come back to Islam. I realized that he was in a quandary, wanting to please the religious leaders and, at the same time, wanting to please us. As I look back on his concerns, his basic fear was for the honor of our family, which in our Islamic society is more important than the right, or even the life, of an individual in the family.

As he tried to dissuade us from our new religion, his mother again reminded him of the tremendous change in my life. There was nothing in Islam that could change a person the way Jesus had changed me. Shafeeq had to acknowledge what she said was true, but he also was concerned that our family name not be dishonored. He kept trying in various ways to discourage me from reading the Bible, while I kept encouraging him to attend Christian meetings, so he could learn for himself about the new life we enjoyed. At that time he had absolutely no desire to attend such meetings.

"But God..."

In 1965, there was an evangelistic campaign sponsored by a church in Khaur, some twenty-five miles from our village. Bill Dalton, the missionary who earlier had visited our village, was taking a few local Christians to those meetings in his VW microbus. In spite of previous refusals to attend Christian meetings, Shafeeq finally consented to go. It was far enough away that his friends would not know that he was in a Christian meeting.

Pakistani pastors and missionaries gave messages and led Bible studies. Through these exposures to the Scriptures, Shafeeq began to comprehend who Jesus really is—and it had its effect! One night after hearing a challenging message, he talked with Bill Dalton.

"I saw something tonight I never realized before. I now understand that Jesus really did shed his blood for me, a sinner. I want to ask him to forgive me of my sins." That night he also became a follower of Jesus Christ, as Bill led him in a prayer of confession of faith in the Lord Jesus.

Bill noticed a religious amulet on a string around Shafeeq's neck and asked, "Does this help you?" Shafeeq answered negatively, so Bill suggested he remove it, which he did. Bill then showed him from the Bible that Jesus himself provides for our needs, and that trusting in amulets is like trusting idols, which are an abomination for both Muslims and Christians.

Attending these Christian meetings also helped me mature spiritually. As I compared the joy of my new life in Christ with the lack of happiness in my life without Jesus, my heart overflowed with praise for my Lord and Savior. The special meetings and fellowship bolstered my assurance that I was heaven bound, an assurance I had never experienced in Islam.

Sometime later Shafeeq and I attended meetings in Attock City, in which a Pakistani Bible teacher, Laal Deen, was the speaker. He was a walking concordance and could quote verses from memory to answer innumerable questions about the Bible. His knowledge of the Bible was fantastic and greatly influenced both of us. In one meeting, he spoke about water baptism. After his explanation of baptism there was no doubt in our minds how we should respond.

Yes, I had heard about baptism some time before and understood it to be a step of obedience for Christians, but I never pressed the matter. In my own mind, I had a reason for putting it off. I had asked the Lord that both Zubeda and Shafeeq be saved before I was baptized. God wonderfully answered that prayer.

Bill Dalton invited Bill Pietsch, a TEAM missionary from Abbottabad, to baptize us. He traveled some sixty miles over hilly roads for the baptismal service. Many Christian in our area gathered on the sandy banks of the Haro River, near Attock City. Colorful, long head coverings worn by the women added to the beauty of the setting. Tall grass at the edge of the water swayed with the gentle breeze that kept the temperature comfortable for the occasion. It was a beautiful scene. Tears of joy ran down numerous cheeks, as we individually emerged from the water. Everyone in attendance was aware of the miracle lives standing before them dripping wet. In the joy of the moment they broke into an Urdu song of praise for our Savior.

I had known for some time that I was saved and belonged to Jesus, but after my baptism, I presented myself afresh to the Lord with a desire to serve him more whole-heartedly. I had to confess, however, that at times I became angry and used language not fitting for a Christian. But each time I slipped back into my old habits, the Spirit of God convicted me and I would confess my sin. As per his promise, he never left me—even when I wondered off the path he set for me.

Another safeguard in my Christian life was the way our children recognized and responded to my slipping into old habits. Whenever there an argument in our home, one of the children would bring me the Bible to read. One verse was of special help: "If we confess our sins, he is faithful and just and will forgive us our sins and purify us from all unrighteousness" (John 1:9). With such a promise from God's Word in my hand, my anger would always abate. I shared this testimony several times, and it always had a profound effect on fellow followers of the Lord Jesus.

The more I saw of the "Christian" community, the more I noticed that most Christians try to ignore the need to confess sin. They hope in some way their guilt will simply go away. Little wonder that there are so many weak Christians! They either are not acquainted with God's Word or else they simply refuse to obey it. But I want my life to be an example for such people; therefore, I try to obey what I learn from God's word.

Another way to express my commitment to Jesus Christ was when I changed my name from Mehmood Shah Qureshi to Mehmood Masih Qureshi. I told the postmaster of the change in my name and in my new address. My new address was simply "Masih House (Christ House), Pind Sultani." To make sure the post office would acknowledge this new address, I sent myself a letter from another village and was delighted that it reached me!

As letters began to arrive at my new address, I noticed that envelopes were being opened. One of my close relatives worked at the post office. I learned that it was he who took it upon himself to "examine" my mail. As he read things written about Jesus Christ and the Christian life, he spread word around the village of the terrible things people were writing to me. Again, it was the name of Jesus Christ that was offensive. If only I would not have used that name so much! But I could not keep from using it. It meant so much to me. The name of Jesus was more precious to me than any name that has ever be used on earth or in heaven above. I know it has power to change human hearts, for it changed mine!

As people became more aware of my genuine commitment to Christ, they gladly participated in the boycott against our family. Getting groceries and other essentials from other villages was not too great a problem; water was hard to transport on the motorcycle.

"But God…"

I had turned to God for help many times, so it was natural that I ask him to solve this problem. As I prayed, the thought of digging a well in our courtyard entered my mind, but it seemed too far-fetched to be practical—until I unexpectedly met a friend of Bill Dalton's, who was a Shia Muslim. This man understood our predicament, because Shias are also a minority in Pakistan and also face discrimination at times.

When he heard about the boycott, he said, "Qureshi, go ahead and dig a well in your courtyard. I will pay for it."

Although I did not accept this man's offer, some Christian brothers encouraged me to go ahead and dig a well in our courtyard. We did, and struck very good-tasting water! This got the attention of everyone in the village.

Our family greatly rejoiced in the Lord's provision of our own well, and before long we had another opportunity to demonstrate Christian love. The village well went dry! Could you believe it? The very people who would not let us use their well now had no water for themselves! I could have gloated over a personal vindication with my neighbors, but Jesus asked me, "What would I do?"

In John 4:10, Jesus invited thirsty ones to come to him and drink. "If you knew the gift of God, and who it is who says to you, 'Give me a drink,' you would have asked him, and he would have given you living water." I did the same thing—except the water I offered could satisfy only physical thirst. Nevertheless, we followed the words of Jesus: "…love your enemies; do good to those who hate you" (Luke 6:27).

On the sly a few women did come for water from our secluded courtyard, even though none of the men would stoop to such a thing. When women came, our daughters often helped by pulling up buckets of water for them. At times Zubeda served tea to the ladies. She even helped them wash clothes in our courtyard. It was a wonderful opportunity for us to show the love of Jesus to women who had never known a true Christian. All these women had ever heard about Christianity were negative comments given by their fathers, husbands, and *imams*. Now they could compare what they saw in our family with their negative ideas about Christianity.

The sympathy the village women had for us was more than the *imam* could stand. He tried to stop everyone from associating with our family, and they knew he meant business.

One Friday, when many men were gathered for the weekly prayers in the mosque, he sternly warned them, "I've been telling you for some time not to have any contact with this Christian family. How can you say your prayers after washing clothes with water from an infidel? You will not be ceremonially clean for prayers if you use their water. These are enemies of Allah and our prophet. They are reprobates with whom we must have absolutely no contact."

Abdul Rehman, one of my distant relatives, had rented land some distance from the village and was away from home when local women began to use water from our well. The next Friday, however, Abdul Rehman was home and heard what these women were doing.

The *imam* knew he had a strong personality and was well respected in the village, so after Friday prayers, the *imam* pointed to him and said, "If Abdul Rehman had been here, none of these women would have been allowed to get water from the infidel's house."

This fed the pride of Abdul Rehman, who quickly stood and boldly addressed the group.

"Imam Sahib, what you have said is true. Unfortunately, I wasn't here to prevent our women from using the infidel's well. But here's what I will do. I have to spend eight days harvesting in a nearby field I rented. However, if eight men will go with me tomorrow, we can finish the work in one day. By tomorrow evening we will return and I guarantee that none of our women will go into the courtyard of this renegade. If they do, I will see to it that their legs are broken."

"But God ... "

Oh the pride and power of local bigwigs! But oh the plans and purposes of Almighty God!

When Abdul Rehman and his men reached the field the next day, the owner of the field met him with three thousand rupees, "I'd be pleased if you would take this money to cover your cost of rent and the crop. My own men will harvest the wheat in a few days."

This angered Abdul Rehman, who said, "If I had come by myself, it would be a deal. But I have come with these men whom I have already paid, so the work can be done quickly. I cannot take the money. My honor is at stake in this matter. We will do the work we came to do." The two men began yelling at each other. Their voices got louder and louder, and a scuffle ensued. Abdul Rehman's anger reached the boiling point. He swung at his agitator with a hand axe. It made a deep opening in the left side of the skull and sliced down into the neck. He died on the spot. As Abdul stood there with his bloody axe, his wife, who had heard the commotion, came to investigate.

"Who killed this man?"

"Your husband," a nearby observer answered.

She was a sickly person. Even though she was accustomed to Abdul Rehman's harsh and unreasonable actions at times, such news was too much for her.

"Why did he have to do something like this?"

Knowing her husband would have to go to jail for his behavior, she began to wail. Abdul Rehman, already angered and taken back by what he had just done, grabbed her by the throat and threw her down.

Within minutes she was dead. Needless to say, he did not return the next day to prevent the women from getting water from our well.

I heard of that terrible story from one of our daughters, who lived near the scene. She had over-heard everything and gave me the details. I was sorry it ended that way, but thankful that God had once again prevented an adversary from getting the upper hand.

This story of Abdul Rehman reminded me of an interesting incident in the Old Testament. King Sennacherib threatened to destroy Jerusalem, and he certainly had the power to do so. *But God* prevented the destruction as found in 2 Kings 19:32–36 (be sure to read this fascinating story of God's overruling the strongest ruler on earth).

> He shall not come to this city or shoot an arrow there; neither shall he come before it with a shield, nor throw up a mound against it ... I will defend this city to save it for my own sake.

Our Christian friends were pleased that God had stopped Abdul Rehman from hindering my efforts to make the name of Jesus known in my village. I assured them, however, that my wife and I would be praying for Abdul Rehman's family. From the depths of our hearts, we wanted to obey the words of Jesus in Matthew 5:14: "Love your enemies and pray for those who persecute you." I wanted everyone to know that Abdul Rehman was not opposing me; he was opposing Jesus Christ. It was the name of Jesus Christ that offended him, not the name of Qureshi. I also explained that, unless God would allow it, he did not have any power to stop my efforts to live for Jesus.

How wonderful that God overrules the plans of men anytime he desires. He did it time and again throughout Scripture, and he has done it time and again for me. At times when God allowed us to have sickness, accidents, and death, I learned this valuable lesson: God is in control during times of trouble as much as he is in control when all goes according to our desires.

BEING AN EVANGELIST

For many years, I was a reporter for a local Urdu newspaper, which meant that I traveled a lot. I used busses to get to rural areas to obtain herbs with which I made medicines. When traveling in and around the Islamabad-Rawalpindi areas, I usually rode my 125cc motorcycle.

During bus trips I often found opportunities to talk about Jesus and the Bible. During one of these trips, I found a seat and pulled out my carefully wrapped Bible. Those sitting near me noticed something different when they eyed the book I was reading. It looked like a holy book, but it was not green, as is the normal color of the Quran.

Had I been reading the Quran, fellow travelers would have paid no attention, but my book looked different and provoked the question, "What are you reading?"

*While Qureshi was reading the Bible on a bus, a
fellow passenger threatened to shoot him.*

"This is the Holy Bible that contains the books of Moses, of David, and of Jesus Christ that Muslims are instructed to read. Have you ever read them?" My question often led into interesting conversations.

One time, however, a fellow passenger perked up his ears when he found a "Muslim" reading the Christians' holy book.

When he learned that I really was a Christian, he blurted out so all could hear, "You should be shot."

I usually carried a holstered pistol when traveling, so in response I pulled out my pistol, offered it to him and said, "Okay. Go ahead and shoot me." This silenced the offended man and amused fellow passengers.

I always found ways to tell about Jesus and what he had done for me. In explaining the good news about Jesus Christ to Muslims, I tried to show real concern and love for them. In Matthew I read that we are to love our enemies, and that God gives us the grace to do this. He has forgiven us so much that I found real joy in showing his love to others. I also noticed something interesting. When men meet with me alone, they usually are cordial and friendly. But in a crowd, it's a different story. They either ignore me or start a noisy argument.

I remember the time I was going home on my motorcycle and met a neighbor carrying a load of wood on his shoulder. I offered to take him on the motorcycle. He arranged his load on the rack behind him, and we soon arrived at his village. As we reached his house, I started to turn in, but he said, "It's better that you stop here. I'll take the load from this point, for if my family saw you, they wouldn't understand." I knew what he meant, so I left him and went on my way. Once again, I did not take the incident personally, for I realized the villagers' animosity was not against me, but against my Savior.

A Drainage Project

Throughout large areas of Pakistan, dry riverbeds are a feature of the landscape. For most of the year they remain dry, but during heavy rains they can become rushing torrents. Where minor roads cross them, the government usually builds a concrete slab that allows traffic to continue during light rains. During heavy rains they are impassable.

Our village used to have a dry riverbed, but due to the conniving of a greedy farmer, it filled with dirt and no longer was able to handle the flow of water in our village. Because of it was full of dirt, one flood heavily damaged thirty houses and swept two children to their death when they drowned in the rushing water. Since most village houses are made with mud walls, flood damage is extensive and expensive. Such losses would not have happened had the riverbed not been filled in. Finally, the men in the village had had enough. They wanted action. Since I was working as a reporter for the local newspaper, the villagers asked me to document the damage for publication in the paper.

I was a reporter for an Urdu newspaper, but I also felt compassion for those who had lost so much and was eager to help. In evaluating the situation, I realized the necessary work would not be done unless someone "took the bull by the horns." I decided to be that person.

To expedite things I personally went to the necessary offices. In spite of my efforts nothing was done for the next two months. (I had no intention of using the customary "oil" of bribery to get the machinery of bureaucracy running.) Out of frustration I pleaded with the village leaders, "I, as a Christian, want to help you. Don't you, as Muslims, have any desire to help your own people?"

Because of this challenge they arranged for the District Commissioner (commonly called the DC; he is the top civilian administrator in a district) to make a personal visit to the area. When they approached him, they learned that he had already read my article in the paper and was willing to look into the problem. His concern worked wonders. Many volunteers showed up to offer their help and to see that something was done.

I explained to the DC that when I was younger, this dry riverbed handled the flood waters, and there was never any flooding. The trouble came after a selfish farmer gradually plowed closer and closer to the edge of the dry riverbed. As it slowly filled in, this farmer gained more tillable land.

I explained that if the riverbed were cleaned and restored to its original condition, the problem of flooding would be solved.

"But who will pay for it?" the DC inquired.

I replied, "The government."

"Was it the government's fault that it was filled in?"

"Oh no. It's the fault of this Haji Sahib," as I pointed to the political leader of the village.

The DC could hardly believe his ears. A despised Christian who had converted from Islam was accusing one of the most influential men in the village—even in front of a government official! The average villager would not dare do what I had just done. But I explained it just as it had happened, for I had personally witnessed the gradual filling in of the dry riverbed by this rascal. I then pointed out the former boundaries of the riverbed so everyone could see how wide it used to be. I explained that the Haji Sahib had hired people to fill it in, so he could have more tillable land.

Again the DC was astonished with my boldness and clarity, especially in the presence of the esteemed, but guilty, village leader.

The DC interjected and told the men listening to my story, "This village needs a man like Qureshi among you!"

I immediately replied, "But I do live among them."

The DC bantered, "But you really should become a Muslim."

I pointed to the man who was the cause of the problem and said, "You mean like that man?"

"No, not like him," replied the DC as he continued the banter. "But if I lived here, I would convince you to become a Muslim again."

The DC's reply prompted me to present the Bible I had brought for the occasion. I explained to him, "This book is the reason for the great change in my own life. It tells what God had done through Jesus Christ to forgive me of all my sins and to give me a new life, a spiritual life. As we both know you cannot make me a Muslim, nor can I make you a Christian. But if you read this book, you will see what God can do for you."

"Who will explain it to me?"

With a smile I replied, "I will."

As he took the Bible, I explained that it contains the books of Moses, the Psalms of David, and the story of Jesus Christ.

He took the Bible and looked at me in amazement. How could a villager with such initiative and ability have become a Christian? But he did admit that I was different from any Christian he had ever known—and definitely different from the Muslims in that village.

With momentum gained from the DC's visit, work soon began on cleaning out the dry riverbed. To further prove my offer to help was genuine, I was instrumental in getting help to remove dirt from the riverbed. A group of interested men from the village joined me in appealing to the government for aid. In addition, several people from the village gave money from their own pockets. I encouraged a contractor to use his bulldozer for the bulk of the work. With the combined effort of so many, the riverbed was restored to its original boundaries, and the villagers no longer lived in fear of the next gully washer. Yet, in spite of my help for the village, many were displeased that a Christian among them would get credit for heading up the project. Some accused me of repairing the riverbed with money from missionaries, despite the fact that they knew their accusation was false.

After the riverbed was repaired, a longstanding missionary friend, David Mitchell, came for a visit.

I told him, "Brother, I want you to drive in this dry riverbed from one end to the other as a way of celebrating what the Lord has done for these people."

There would be no more flooded houses or children washed downstream. What a relief! This all came about because I had learned how to respond to opposition and ridicule—by loving and helping my "enemies."

"I was in prison, and you came to me" (Matthew 25:36)

Shortly after my first marriage, I spent time in prison due to my own cunning. Much later, instead of being a prisoner, I was on the outside of the bars visiting a prisoner who was in jail because of his faith in Jesus Christ.

Sher Rehman and his wife lived in the beautiful Swat Valley north of where I lived. They came in contact with the Good News while he was a patient in the Taxila Mission Hospital, some ninety miles southeast of Swat. As a result he, and later his wife, became followers of the Lord Jesus Christ. The Good News of Jesus met a need they had felt for some time. They wanted a God of love, a God who forgives sin. As they read the Bible and heard it explained, they experienced the words of Jesus in John 3:7, "You must be born again."

After they received eternal life in Jesus by the new birth, they still had questions. The Bible, spiritual life, Christian fellowship, all of this was new to them. By God's planning they heard there were Christians in Attock City, which was closer than the mission hospital they had attended. Sher Rehman gladly traveled there to learn more of his new life in Christ. When he heard that missionaries lived in Attock City, he wanted to talk with them, for he assumed they would know more about the Bible than local Christians. Furthermore, he had heard that Pakistani Christians were suspicious of converts from Islam.

Don and Ruth Stoddard lived in Attock City and were glad to help Sher Rehman and his wife grow in their Christian faith. They developed a close relationship with them and even visited their home in Swat a few times. They had to limit their visits, however, because too many visits could have caused trouble for Sher Rehman. Residents in that beautiful valley were accustomed to seeing foreign tourists strolling along and taking pictures of their luscious green valleys and their snow covered mountains. They actually welcomed tourists, because tourism fed the economy of the valley in summer months. But to see foreigners regularly visit a local home would raise all sorts of questions.

Pakistani Christians are less conspicuous than foreigners in the Swat Valley, but even we had to be careful. A Pakistani pastor, George Gill, had been a great help to Sher when Sher was in the Taxila Mission Hospital. Under his teaching, Sher even learned the meaning of baptism., and Pastor George had the privilege of baptizing him. However, due to their strict Islamic background and surroundings his wife was not baptized. One question remained: who could baptize her?

Further contact with the Stoddards proved helpful in this decision. They arranged for Mrs. Sher to be baptized at TEAM's hospital north of Abbottabad, where a Canadian surgeon had built a wading pool for the children of expatriate hospital staff. It was an ideal location for baptisms in a Muslim area, because it was tucked in behind a brick garage some distance from the flow of hospital patients. A sturdy line of hedges walled off the edges of the pool area.

On the appointed date, the Stoddards brought Sher Rehman and his wife the eighty miles to TEAM's hospital. Only a few invited Christian staff witnessed something they had never seen before: a woman baptizing a woman. Some of the Christian staff had questions, because they understood from Scripture that only men are qualified to baptize. However, considering the background of Mrs. Sher Rehman it seemed best that a woman baptize her. Ruth Stoddard had volunteered to do the job, which proved to be a blessing to Sher and his wife.

Sher Rehman continued visiting Don Stoddard as often as possible for spiritual encouragement and guidance. On one of his visits I showed up unexpectedly at the Stoddards' house. I had never met Sher Rehman before, and Don could see the questioning looks we had for each other. Brother Don kept the conversation moving, so we could become a bit acquainted. His easy-going method proved to be the needed icebreaker, and a trusting friendship soon developed. I was able to bolster Sher's faith in the Lord, for I had experienced the ruthless opposition Sher Rehman would face.

Less than .2% of the population of Swat Valley were Christian, so the locals were greatly disturbed when one of their own became a Christian. As far as they knew, the only Christians in their gloriously beautiful valley were foreigners or lowly sweepers.

When people learned that Sher Rehman and his wife had become Christians, the opposition began. Time in jail was part of what they endured for their faith in the Lord Jesus Christ.

When Pastor George heard of their predicament, he made the three-hour bumpy bus ride to the Swat Valley to visit Sher and his wife and to encourage them. He had hoped to obtain their release, but his efforts were useless.

"But God…"

I also heard of their confinement and I, too, made a special trip to visit them. With my knowledge of Islam I soon struck up a conversation with some of the prison personnel, and somehow God used my visit to have them released. They were so thankful to the Lord for their new acquaintance and his concern.

I was impressed with God's plan for this isolated couple and wondered how many more lived in secluded areas whom God has chosen before the foundations of the earth. We'll never know unless someone goes and tells them the Good News.

For this couple, God used their medical problem to draw them to a place they could hear about Jesus Christ. He also had prepared their hearts for the Good News of Jesus Christ. From all I know, Rehman and his wife remained firm in their new life in Christ Jesus as two of very few Christians in that valley.

BEING A GOOD SAMARITAN

My neighbors could not reconcile their memories of me before I accepted Christ with what they saw in me in their days of sickness. They used to consider me mentally unbalanced, for I cursed God and cared for no one, yet here I was "clothed and in my right mind" and doing for them what they could not do for themselves. As a registered dispenser of herbal medicines, I even provided them with herbal medicines without charge.

As I helped my neighbors, I explained that, regardless of their animosity, I was their friend. I offered the use of any of my tools they needed. I was glad that relatives and neighbors could visibly see what Christ had done for me. Even though they appreciated my efforts, they were not willing to acknowledge that Jesus was the source of the radical changes in my life.

At one point, the effect of my work seemed to backfire. A carpenter named Yaseen wanted the religion I had embraced and declared that he was a Christian. Hearing this, the local *imam* immediately evicted him from his living quarters and took him to the mosque and pressured him to renounce this new religion and return to the ways of Islam. This was more than he could stand. He confessed his "error" in the mosque and started saying his prayers five times a day along with other faithful Muslims in his village.

This young man had failed to notice the price my family had paid for taking such a step and how we had responded to opposition. He did not know Jesus' warning and encouragement in John 16:33: "In this world you will have oppression and tribulation ... but take courage! I have overcome the world." I did not give up hope for Yaseen and continued visiting him from time to time.

I knew Yaseen feared the *imams* and their ability to make things difficult for anyone leaving Islam. He once told me, "If only my wife were alive, I would have been more able to withstand the troubles like you do; but being alone makes it difficult. Even my children and grandchildren helped force me back to Islam."

A Muslim neighbor later opined that if Yaseen hadn't let it be known so quickly that he had become a Christian, he would not have had such trouble. Then he added something I found profound and encouraging. "It's quite likely that others also would have become Christians, if only he had been more discreet in talking about Christianity." Did this neighbor and possibly others have an inclination to learn more about God's wonderful plan of salvation?

Road building: Physical and Spiritual

I was constantly amazed how God provided opportunities for me to talk about Jesus because of my concern for people. For example, I had the chance to help a contractor who was rebuilding roads after heavy rains. After watching the rather sluggish way he was getting dirt to build up the roadbed, I suggested a better method, which saved the contractor time and money. Sometime later I was riding my bicycle near the area. The contractor happened to see me and asked me to stop a moment. He thanked me profusely for all my help and added that it was regretful that I had become an enemy of the true religion. I explained that I did not intend to offend anyone, but that it was not a hasty decision. Only after much thought and prayer did I make the decision. I knew it would affect my family and my relationships with many people. I told him I made that decision because I had found in Jesus Christ something Islam does not offer—the assurance of forgiveness of sin and of heaven.

To get the point across I probed, "Does Islam offer this type of assurance?" He admitted that a Muslim has no way knowing for sure whether he will be in heaven or not.

He put it this way: "No one, I mean no one, can know that until the judgment day. Anyone who claims such knowledge is a puffed-up fool."

Following that bold statement the contractor quietly confided to me.

"Let's leave that for now, for I want to tell you something I've shared with very few people. I once had a dream in which I saw a road going from my house and stretching far into the distance. It was paved with white crushed stone. In the dream I asked who was building that road and was told that you were the builder." How the Lord worked me into that dream I'll never know, but the dream added credibility to my testimony.

Even though the contractor showed no more interest in forgiveness through Jesus Christ, he had heard biblical teaching he had never heard before. I know that if Jesus Christ does not bring this man to himself, that's his work and his alone. But I won't be surprised if I see him in heaven someday. In fact, many of us might be surprised at those we find in heaven, some who seemed hopeless cases as we talked to them about Jesus here on earth.

More Persecution

After my mother had a stroke, I visited her many times with no problems from the family. She was so glad to have me visit that every time I started to leave, she insisted that I stay longer. Unfortunately that was not possible, since I had responsibilities at home. It was only two days after my last visit I heard from my son-in-law that Mother had died.

Before this I had experienced the effects of various kinds of boycotts, but I had no idea boycotts could go beyond merely cutting off food and water supplies. My son Shafeeq and I went with my son-in-law to view my mother's body. When we were ready to go into the room where her body lay, my stepfather and son-in-law took me aside.

"The men of the village have decided you will not be able to see your mother's face, unless you fulfill one condition. You must say in front of everyone present that you had made a mistake in leaving Islam. Your confession must include a denial of the false religion you accepted plus an affirmation that you will follow the prophet of Islam and all his teaching. This will satisfy our Muslim brotherhood. We personally know you will not change your mind, but for the sake of the occasion, you should agree with this demand. Afterward you can go back to your new religion or anything else you desire. The confession could be a temporary thing."

I explained that it was impossible for me to deny the Lord Jesus, even for a brief moment, because of all he had done for me. The men then told me in no uncertain words that I would not be allowed to see my mother's face before they buried her. This brought tears to my eyes, but I made it clear that it was more important to remain true to my Savior than see my mother's face one last time. I explained that it was only her body they would bury. They would put only her body in the ground to return to dirt from which it was made—and that would be it! She could not recognize me or respond to my voice.

My stepfather asked, "You mean you do not honor the mother who gave you birth, who nursed you, who cared for you as you grew up?"

I assured him that I greatly respected my mother and was thankful for all she had done for me, but that I could not express that to her body, which was all that was left. I further explained, "The Injeel tells of a woman who said to Jesus, 'Blessed is the womb that bore you, and the breasts at which You nursed.' Jesus gave an unexpected reply, 'On the contrary, blessed are those who hear the word of God, and observe it.'

"It's true that the Quran and the Injeel give Mary great honor, but Jesus emphasized that knowing and obeying God's Word is greater than any honor we can give a human being. My purpose in life is to obey his Word as completely as I can.

"On the other hand, I want you to remember that when I was a Muslim you knew I didn't believe in God. You saw how I easily became angry and cursed God. In those days you did nothing to correct me, but now that I follow Jesus Christ and have found peace and joy in him, you want me to change. I don't understand it. I wouldn't exchange the peace of heart and assurance in Jesus for anything. I just wish you could understand what Jesus did for me—and can do for you."

My words, however, fell on deaf ears, and the funeral soon began. My stepfather joined the other men in the procession to take the body to the grave-yard. As they carried the wooden box, Shafeeq and I sat on a balcony in my daughter's house and watched. After the procession reached the grave, we heard the *imam* recite the prescribed portions of the Quran and watched from a distance, as the men lined up in rows facing Mecca and said the prescribed prayers. Then, with ropes reaching under the box and held by men on both sides of the grave, they slowly lowered my mother's body into the grave and began to fill it with handfuls of dirt. After everyone had tossed in a handful, the diggers used shovels to complete the job. We watched. Our eyes filled with tears—but our hearts were at peace.

✝

After the burial something strange happened. Shafeeq and I were sitting with the men in the court-yard when a young fellow appeared selling religious booklets. For some reason, he came directly to me and pleaded for me to buy one of the booklets. I told him several times that I did not need the books and would not buy any.

Finally, he leaned down and whispered in my ear, "Someone picked my pocket and I have no money." He begged for two rupees to have at least one meal.

I reiterated that I would not take any of the booklets but I did tell him that I would arrange for food to be brought from inside. The young man ate his fill and left.

After the meal, men gathered empty plates to put in a tub for washing, but my sister interrupted, "Who was that young salesman?" The reason for her question was that Christians were known for going through villages selling literature, and she assumed he was a Christian. Because the young man singled me out, everyone else also assumed that he was a Christian—even though I knew he was a Muslim.

My sister assessed the situation and didn't allow the men to put the salesman's plate in the tub for washing, "We cannot mix dishes used by an infidel with those used by true believers."

I interjected, "You mean that because my son and I are Christians, our plates should not be washed in that tub either?"

My sister took advantage of that opening. "Let me put it this way; we will have many guests in the next few days, and many think it better that you not be here. Changing your religion is a great dishonor to the memory of our mother. Yes, it would be better that you both leave." Following those scorching words, we left.

After the trauma of our mother's death, my sister and brother-in-law tried very hard to prevent me from receiving any of the inheritance. However, a judge ruled that I was to get half of it, my sister a quarter, and my stepfather a quarter. Even then my relatives tried to hinder this plan. Their dander was still up.

To help settle the dust I had an idea to which they agreed. This involved some land that I offered to sell to my sister for 30,000 rupees. She agreed and paid 25,000 rupees with the balance to be paid later.

An Unexpected Attack

I had seen the Lord intervene in many situations, as I faced taunts and threats of those trying to get me to return to Islam. God had proven himself so faithful and far beyond anything I could have expected. When a jab came from a fellow Christian, however, it took me by complete surprise. This actually hurt more than attacks by Muslims. When I was a babe in Christ, a pastor made a cutting remark, which I later learned expressed the sentiments of many in the Christian community.

"What does he want from us anyway? These 'converts' always have an ulterior motive. Why does he have to come to us and cause trouble?"

Cutting? Very much so! I later learned there really are many examples of those who pretend to become a Christian only to get money, a job, learn English, or even a wife. Unfortunately, this pastor had seen only this kind of "conversion," and was rightfully fed up with them. I was completely unaware of such cases and was devastated by the false accusation.

This accusation upset me so much that I was about to leave the faith. Fortunately my daughter, Sameena, came to the rescue. She knew me very well, for her personality is much like mine. From that vantage point, she calmly explained the reason for the cutting remark. She reminded me that in comparison to all Jesus had suffered for us, the pastor's remark was inconsequential. She pointed out that God was using his remark to make me more like Jesus.

"Read Romans 8:28–29 again," she urged, "and you'll see this is true."

I gratefully accepted that explanation and was ready to take the insult as a God-appointed step in my becoming a more mature Christian. It was almost as if God was saying, "I want you to take that cutting remark as from me." That thought hit me like a bolt out of the blue! But it proved to be a solid anchor that helped me many, many times. I was beginning to see to what extent the loving sovereignty of God extends.

That pastor stayed aloof from me for some time, but he kept hearing about my life from several Christians. He even unobtrusively observed me over a period of time and finally realized his error. When he was convinced that I truly was his brother in Christ, he apologized and became a close friend.

Daughter's Marriage

Shameem, a daughter from my first marriage, had been of marriageable age for some time, so there was talk that we should make wedding arrangements for her. Some suggested she marry a cousin, a common practice in Pakistan. However, I found another possibility more to my liking.

I observed a young man during a trip to the Christian hospital in Taxila to visit a friend with a broken leg. Most hospitals in Pakistan require patients to bring at least one relative to care for the patient's personal needs. The relative who accompanied my friend listened intently to the preaching by a local pastor, as he daily explained the Good News of Jesus to patients. He began to show interest.

As I became somewhat acquainted with the man, I thought we should approach his parents about a marriage arrangement. Since he showed so much interest in the Gospel, I thought he might be a possible mate for Shameem. (At this point I had not learned the admonition in 2 Cor. 6:14 that believers are not to marry unbelievers.) However, when this young fellow's father heard of it, he flatly refused and wanted nothing to do with the idea. He could not stand the thought of having a daughter-in-law who was a Christian. I was discouraged, but still thought it workable and pressed the matter a bit further. My efforts were useless. Even a judge sided with the father, which reinforced the father's refusal to agree on a marriage arrangement.

Still, I continued to think the idea was feasible, so I sent the judge a note quoting Sura 5:5, which says that Muslims are permitted to marry women who are "people of the book" (Jews and Christians). The judge backpedaled a bit and admitted, "I am well aware of the verse to which you refer. So—since you brought it up, I would be willing to perform the wedding ceremony and also to persuade the father that it does not violate our holy book."

Wedding plans were back on track. One of my nephews was greatly displeased with the plan and tried to dissuade people from attending. His efforts failed, because word had already spread about the wedding—and everyone knows that where there's a wedding, there's food!

The wedding was performed, but the marriage did not last very long. Under pressure, the *imam* soon annulled the wedding and announced his decision from the mosque. He also arranged for Shameem's new husband, Jalil, to be accused of becoming a Christian. As a result, Jalil was beaten and was under such pressure that he asked for a divorce.

But there was more. Someone stole the wedding presents. I mentioned this to the judge, because he had authority to order an investigation. He calmly told me to forget it, for he could not control things under such circumstances.

It was soon learned that Jalil himself had taken the presents. To get attention away from himself he tried to cause a disagreement between his own father and me. But we two fathers had come to a mutual understanding. In fact, I had given his father 3,000 rupees to help with expenses.

But then, Jalil, who proved to be a real rascal, stole that money from his father. As people heard about this boy's actions, they shook their heads and quoted an Urdu proverb that is equivalent to "there's a fox in a henhouse." Since he and his family were Muslims, his actions were a great dishonor for his family.

Three days later, Bill Dalton came for a worship service in my house. After the service someone saw his VW van leaving the village with his big dog in the back seat. From the silhouette people saw in the dim evening light, they assumed it was a blanket hiding wedding presents and that Bill was taking them away from the village to remove incriminating evidence from me. This idea fit in well with their hope of implicating me in the theft of the presents. This rumor spread in spite of the fact that the boy's father had already reported to the police that his own son had stolen the presents and that I was not involved.

Since the rumor was making its rounds in the village, a police officer heard the name of Mahmood Masih as a possible suspect and had me brought in for questioning. I appeared in court, and the judge called for "Mahmood Masih" to come before the bench.

I stepped forward, and the judge asked with a look of surprise on his face, "What are you doing here?"

"You called me," I nonchalantly replied.

"But your name isn't Mahmood Masih, is it?"

The judge knew me as a newspaper reporter Mahmood Shah, not Mahmood Masih. The name change raised his eyebrow, but he was even more surprised that I had given my daughter to a family of such questionable character.

I briefly explained the situation but quickly added, in defense of Bill Dalton, "The foreigner that people told you about is a missionary, and you can rest assured that he was not involved in the theft."

The judge then turned to the father of the thief.

"I will see that justice is done but first you must bring your son to me. When you bring him, then, and then only, will I hear the case. If Qureshi is guilty, he will be punished; but until your son appears, I will do nothing further about this case."

There were several who vouched for me, saying I had done nothing wrong. Even the older police officers who had known me for years were dubious about the accusation. It was marvelous the way the Lord used even these old friendships to rule in my favor.

I was very sorry that things turned out as they did, but I had no way of knowing that the young man who married my daughter was such a scoundrel. But what was done was done. A divorce relieved the situation a bit, but by now there was another factor. During the brief marriage Shameem became pregnant and later gave birth to a son, whom we named Naasar. Because of the divorce there was no father to raise the boy. Zubeda and I realized the gravity of the situation and decided we should raise him. When we applied for guardianship, however, there was a complication. His Muslim relatives objected vehemently to having the child raised in a Christian home.

In discussing the matter with several people a possible solution surfaced. If a 5,000 rupee fine were paid, the child could legally be raised a Christian and could even attend a Christian school. A lawyer drew up the papers, but these papers were in English, which I couldn't understand. I took them to missionary Bill Pietsch, who was then living in Attock City. Bill read the paper and then took me to see a judge with whom he had become acquainted. This judge was very practical and simply advised us to raise the boy until he was of age—but to keep the matter as quiet as possible. We did that and were able to raise Naasar without any complications.

After arrangements were made for us to raise Naasar, we made another wedding arrangement for his mother, Shameem. As Shameem adjusted to her new living arrangement in a Muslim home, one of her new husband's brothers heard about Shameem's younger sister, Aqeela. Would it be possible for him, a Muslim, to marry her? I strongly objected, because by that time I had learned that 2 Cor. 6:14

forbids a Christian from being unequally yoked with unbelievers.

When it was known that Aqeela was to be married to a Christian, there was much opposition in the village. They threatened, "You arranged for Shameem to be married to a Muslim, and you must do the same for Aqeela. We will not let her be married to a Christian!"

"But God…"

Unbeknownst to us the Lord had been working things out for Aqeela 750 miles to the south. Fazal had grown up in a Muslim family in Karachi, but by God's goodness he met a humble Christian tailor who had the courage to talk with him about Jesus Christ.

(Since hearing of that Christian tailor I have observed many times that there are very few Christians who talk about Jesus. They talk about their church or Christian activities, but few Christians talk about Jesus. Jesus means so much to followers of Jesus Christ that we should be compelled to talk about him.)

When Fazal heard about Jesus, he was fascinated.

These simple words grabbed his attention. "Jesus suffered for our sins. He took the punishment that should be ours. Because of his paying the penalty for our sins, he offers forgiveness of sins and eternal life as a gift. Since he paid the price, eternal life is free for the asking." This was an entirely new concept. He had never heard anything close to that in Islam. Such unexpected good news captivated his thoughts.

As he contemplated his future, he suddenly faced the fact that his environment and life in Karachi were leading him nowhere. He had seen many of his buddies' lives ruined. He was ready for a change. In search of satisfaction he earnestly prayed for God to show him the right way. The Lord gave him understanding through fellowship with various Christians. With increased knowledge of the Bible, he reached the point of committing himself to the Lord for salvation. As a new Christian, he was so full of enthusiasm that he joined evangelistic teams as they witnessed for Jesus in Karachi.

He also began trusting God for a job within a Christian environment. That need was met when he learned of the need for a calligrapher in a Christian publishing house in Lahore. (Before computers became common, calligraphers were in much demand, especially for Urdu printing.) The idea of working in a Christian organization thrilled him! He would be able to continue with his profession after all.

After conversations and letters of recommendation, he moved 750 miles north to Lahore and started to work at MIK (Christian Publishing House). God already had another convert from Islam in Lahore, and he was more than ready to help Fazal. Ashraf Paul had come to the Lord some years earlier and was already active in evangelism in Lahore and surrounding areas. When he met Fazal, he at once felt a oneness with him and was eager to encourage him anyway possible.

Later, this Ashraf Paul heard that I was trying to find a suitable arrangement for Aqeela. So, he suggested to the manager of MIK that he should get in touch with me. Fazal had been at MIK long enough that their staff had become personally concerned about a marriage arrangement for him. Their involvement was vital, since his Muslim family in Karachi would have nothing to do with planning a Christian wedding for their son. After the MIK staff contacted me, several of us spent much time in prayer about an arrangement. Not too many days later, we all felt free to make the arrangements.

As wedding plans began, neither I nor anyone else had any idea what sinister forces were working to cause harm and spoil the whole thing. On the other hand, those rogues had no idea of what our sovereign God had in mind!

According to Pakistani custom, the groom's relatives and friends rent a bus and go to the house of the bride for the wedding ceremony. After the ceremony they escort the bride and groom back to the bridegroom's house, where they stay for a few days. At the end of those days the bride returns home for a final farewell by her family.

Troublemakers from Pind Sultani learned of the wedding plans and planned to act. They were going to set fire to the bus carrying the wedding party from Pind Sultani to Lahore. That one-way trip requires at least five hours by bus, so there would be plenty opportunities for them to carry out their deadly plan.

"But God…"

None of us had any idea of their scheme, so we merrily carried on with the arrangements. On the day of the wedding in 1982, there were heavy rains throughout the Punjab Province, and they continued throughout the day. God used these soaking rains to prevent the troublemakers from carrying out their life-threatening scheme. All went as planned. The wedding party arrived in Pind Sultani from Lahore, the wedding was performed, and the wedding party returned safely to the groom's house in Lahore before the rain stopped!

Our Daily Bread

Later in 1982, an announcement blared from the loudspeakers atop the minarets of the mosque in our village.

"No one is to associate with the Qureshi family in any way."

Even my Muslim daughter was warned not to come to our house or deliver milk to us—"not until your father changes." After a couple of days we had nothing but a little whole-wheat flour and a type of greens for our evening meal. There would be nothing left to eat in the morning.

To add to our plight, our newlyweds arrived from Lahore, so we had them to feed as well. Once more these two special words were interjected into the formula for God's provision for our needs.

"But God…"

At 10:15 p.m., we were praying and giving ourselves to the Lord when we heard a motorcycle stop outside the courtyard gate. I took my revolver and went to the door. Instead of an intruder or troublemaker, there was Asif Khan, a dear Christian brother from Abbottabad, some eighty miles away! He had ridden a motorcycle in the rain to bring provisions that David Davis, missionary friend, had purchased for us. This timely answer to prayer was evidence of God's care and helped me so much to grow in my faith. I vowed anew to serve my Lord with my whole heart, for I could testify to those who tried to make things difficult for us that our God knows their schemes and that he cares for his own!

Asif Khan "helping" Qureshi

In the meantime, the *imam* who had instigated most of the trouble was in trouble. He had to get out of our area to save his own skin, so he fled over a hundred miles to a city north of Lahore to avoid punishment for a hidden crime of his own! Another *imam* was brought in to replace the miscreant, but this did not change our situation. This new *imam* agreed with the previous *imam* that anyone who eats with us is not a Muslim! With this *imam,* however, there was another factor: he knew me from previous contacts and had eaten in our home a few times.

Later I asked, "Did you just find out today that I had become a Christian? That was twenty-five years ago!" The *imam* saw he was caught, and sheepishly confided to me, "I will not cause you trouble again."

More Pressure to Recant

In 1983, a very influential *imam* near Lahore offered me one hundred thousand rupees (about ten thousand dollars) along with promises of help my family, if only I would recant and return to Islam. I have known other converts from Islam who would have jumped at this opportunity, but this offer held absolutely no appeal to me. Anything these men offered would not last. What I gained in Jesus Christ will last forever.

The *imam* then announced over the loudspeaker for people to come to the mosque at 2:30 p.m. There they would decide what they should do with one who denies Islam. Many people assembled, for they had heard that the *imam* was going to force me to return to Islam one way or another. Again, God had other plans. The *imam* who had gathered people to witness my "return to Islam" had an accident while harvesting wheat by hand. A piece of straw cut his eye, and he had to go to a hospital. The injury was very serious and resulted in the loss of sight in that eye.

Further Encouragements

Another lesson the Lord has taught is that I need to be aggressive for him at times. Once I was at the police station for questioning about becoming a follower of Jesus, and I initiated a conversation when there was a lull in the questioning. I asked a police officer, "Can you buy faith?"

His answer was not totally unexpected. "That's what missionaries have done with you."

"Quite the contrary. They gave me no money, nor did I follow Jesus for that purpose. They never offered help in getting to another country, and I certainly did not turn to Jesus to get a wife. You undoubtedly have heard of Muslims pretending to become Christians so they will get material benefits. And I have learned there are such cases, but I turned to him for forgiveness from all my sins!

"I know that's hard for you to believe, because Islam teaches that a person can have no assurance of forgiveness for his sins. But let me ask you this: wouldn't it be wonderful, if you could know without doubt that you will go to heaven after you die?" He had to ponder that thought for a while, before dismissing that idea as impossible.

I was so thankful the Lord encouraged me with words to talk about Jesus. It was similar to the way he encouraged his disciples when they were speechless before authorities.

> When they bring you before … the authorities, do not become anxious about what … you should say; for the Holy Spirit will teach you in that very hour what you ought to say.
>
> Luke 12:11–12

Another encouragement for us was by a sympathizer who urged us to stay in the village.

"Don't leave the village. The time will come when many people will believe as you do." It seems this man was a seeker after truth and had seen enough in my life that he wanted it for himself. I never did know whether this man's heart was the type of soil in which the Word would take root and grow or not, but his statement did show me that there were men in our village wanting something they had not found in Islam.

On another occasion the Lord diverted opposition from our family by the sinful conduct of an *imam*. This religious leader was having an affair with a girl. What he was doing in the dark eventually came out in the light, and he became the object of scorn and ridicule.

"You have been saying all these things against the Qureshi family, but you yourself have been carrying on this affair! What kind of *imam* are you?"

Also, there was the time Zubeda visited her father, who was very ill. Her brothers bluntly told her that she could not enter the house, because she was an infidel. They explained that their father had typhoid and was very ill and could not see her.

"But he's my father, and I came to see him. I will not eat anything and certainly will not be staying overnight."

When she learned that her father needed medicine for typhoid, she knew what she had to do. In the past she had suffered from typhoid and had some of the needed medicine in our house, so she went to get it.

When she returned to her father's house, her brothers did not allow her into the house, nor did they take the medicine for their father. She was shocked by their lack of concern for their father. All she could do was to leave the medicine and go back to her own home—in tears.

When her father learned that her brothers did not allow her in the house, he was devastated. Not only did her brothers deny her entrance into their father's home, they did not even give him the medicine she brought for him. Without the needed medicine his condition quickly deteriorated. Three days later he died, but Zubeda had the assurance she had done what she needed to do.

Through all these trials, we never sensed that God had deserted us. All we could do at such times was cling to his promises. Just when we felt we could bear no more hardship, God always intervened in amazing ways.

THE PEANUT
BUTTER ENTERPRISE

Prior to becoming a follower of the Lord Jesus, I had income from various sources: making pickled relish that adds zest to Pakistani food, my herbal medical practice, services performed as a religious teacher, and reporting for an Urdu newspaper. Things changed radically when I became a follower of Jesus Christ. When a Muslim leaves Islam, his family and friends will use any means to pressure him to recant. For us, they used a boycott, which meant that no one was allowed to come to me for herbal medicines, nor for advice in Islam, nor for the pickled relish. I now needed a source of income to provide for the family, but I was not about to turn back. I now had true peace and joy in the Lord Jesus that I had never found before. Nothing could be more precious than that.

As our financial needs loomed larger and larger before us, I again turned to the Lord for guidance, and he answered—in a most unusual way.

A visit to a home in Pakistan guarantees a cup of tea, the national drink of Pakistan. When I paid a visit to Bill Dalton, tea was served, but I noticed something in a small jar on the tray I had never seen before.

I watched him spread this strange-looking concoction on bread and asked, "What's that?"

"It's called peanut butter. It's made from peanuts."

I tried some.

"Hmm! That's good. How do you make it?"

Bill demonstrated by grinding a few roasted peanuts through a meat grinder a couple times. He added a pinch of salt and a few drops of vegetable oil and asked me to try it. I was so impressed that I asked to borrow the grinder. At home I tried my hand at making peanut butter.

"Eureka! It worked!"

The next day I proudly brought some to show the Daltons. Bill was impressed and gave an encouraging response (perhaps with tongue in cheek).

"This tastes better than the peanut butter we brought from the USA."

Bill took a sample of my newly made peanut butter to the residential area for foreigners in Tarbela, where the largest earth-filled dam in the world was being built. There were many Americans among the various nationalities involved in its construction. That was good news for me. As I learned later, most Americans need their peanut butter. This meant there would be several prospective peanut butter customers among those working on that large construction project.

In addition to customers in Tarbela, there was also a ready market in Murree, a former British hill station in the foothills of the Himalayas. During the hot summer months in the plains and desert region's temperatures soar into the 110s and 120s. To avoid the extreme heat, most missionary mothers and their children would move to Murree for three to four months. (Many Pakistanis also seek refuge from the intense heat in the Murree hills.) Their children are able to attend Murree Christian School (MCS) and yet live with their mothers. For part of the summer, fathers gladly join their families.

In the fall, the parents return to their area of work, but their school children stay in Murree and enter the school's boarding arrangement. Those kids have appetites. Many, especially the American children, are great fans of peanut butter, and most love their peanut butter and jelly sandwiches. Since peanut butter was rarely available in the local market, my business would become a reliable source of peanut butter for them. The kids would be able to have their peanut butter and jelly sandwiches, and I would be able to make a living for my family. What a wonderful way the Lord answered prayer!

With so many prospective customers, we needed to get the ball rolling. Bill found an organization in the States that provides technical advice to entrepreneurs in third-world counties. They gladly sent plans for a simple but efficient peanut grinder. With those plans in hand, I found men in the local market to make the grinder. These men knew where to get the necessary parts, and they were very adept in producing what might have been the first peanut grinder in Pakistan. When it was ready, we set it up and started making peanut butter in earnest. Qureshi Peanut Butter was up and running.

After I was getting the swing of it, Bill noticed that I was not washing my hands before making the product nor did I keep the machine and its surroundings clean. Bill explained the importance of cleanliness, so I started keeping the tables and grinder cleaner. I learned to wash my hands each time I started to make peanut butter. With this lesson on hygiene under my belt, I was able to advertise the product as "untouched by human hands" and that it was prepared in "sterile" conditions.

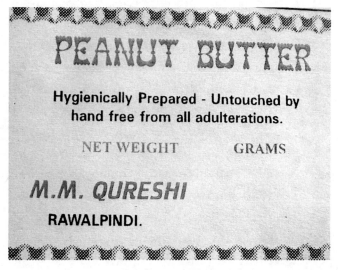

Peanut Butter can label

Bill also helped design the labels to put on the various size and types of containers we used. These containers came mostly from my missionary friends who collected tin cans and glass jars of various sizes. They had been used for cooking oil, jam, canned fruit, etc. I was always delighted to get a fresh supply of containers from my friends, for without their help I would have had to buy containers from scrap dealers in the market or to have used plastic containers that were somewhat expensive. The variety of containers indeed was great, but they all had the Qureshi label that guaranteed natural and tasty peanut butter.

As business increased I purchased large burlap bags full of peanuts, which were plentiful in the local markets, because the sandy ground in our region was just right for raising peanuts. Each bag of roasted peanuts weighed about ninety pounds.

Our whole family got in the act, but work was slow. Even with all family members helping it took us ten days to shell a bagful. I was very aware that God had opened up this means of income, so I turned to God to show a more efficient way to shell the peanuts. And the Lord answered. I woke up during the night with an idea. The following morning another idea came to mind: a cloth-covered roller. This improvement enabled us to shell a bagful of peanuts in just one day, and without as many crushed peanuts as before! What an improvement from the ten days it used to take! Later, even this process was streamlined to the point that we could hull a bag of peanuts in much less time.

One problem remained however. We separated the nuts from the hulls on our flat mud roof, and we could do it only on days when a strong wind could blow away the hulls. Where did the hulls go? Straight into our neighbors' courtyards! This was not a good way to win friends and influence people.

This additional problem forced me into the thinking mode again. How could I prevent the hulls from going into our neighbors' courtyards? It finally dawned on me that an electric fan could provide the needed wind. This would allow us to work inside, and we could do it anytime we wished, wind or no wind.

This innovation made for more contented neighbors, as well as an increased efficiency in processing the peanuts. So, in spite of the boycott by all our neighbors, I now had a reliable source of income. To God be the glory!

✝

My contacts with students of Murree Christian School and their parents proved very helpful when I had an accident on my bicycle in 1984. I was too bruised to harvest the crop I had planted. When this word reached Murree, one of the staff members came up with an idea that proved very helpful for me.

Eleven junior high boys from Murree Christian School, plus a houseparent and a language teacher, came to my rescue. The troupe began picking peanuts after a two and an half hour van ride. It was a beautiful day after a light rain. This welcomed group worked until late in the afternoon. Then they came to my house for an evening meal and to spend the night.

After the meal I gave my testimony of how I came to Jesus. The boys listened attentively, as the language teacher translated into English, but they soon showed signs of weariness. We had prayer, and the boys crawled into their sleeping bags.

While traveling back to Murree the next day, several boys mentioned how they enjoyed my testimony and spending time with my family. I understand it was the first time any of them had spent a night in a Pakistani home.

For most of the boys that trip was the highlight of the school year. For me their visit was a complete surprise, but it was wonderful to see their joy and enthusiasm—and I was so relieved to have two and a half sacks of peanuts picked, since I was not able to do it myself.

Harvesting peanuts with Jonathan Mitchell

✝

Bill Dalton was such a great help throughout the process of getting me set up in the peanut butter business. But that was not all Bill did for me. He also was a spiritual guide and counselor, and, for a bit of icing on the cake, he taught me a bit of etiquette so I would be less "villagey" when eating in homes of expatriates!

One time, I was in a foreigner's house having a meal with the family. At the end of the meal the hostess put a plate of oranges on the table. I looked over the stack of oranges, reached to the other side of the plate and took the largest one. Bill later explained that it is proper to take that which is closest, even though it might be smaller. I looked back on that experience years later as not only humorous, but as a needed lesson that served me well in future situations requiring western "etiquette."

As news of Qureshi Peanut Butter spread (excuse the pun) we received orders from various places. Some of our friends served as distribution points by keeping a case of peanut butter on hand at all times. This was a convenience not only for us but also for expatriates living near those distribution points in various parts of the country.

On one occasion, Don Stoddard drove me to Murree in the winter to deliver a large order of peanut butter to Murree Christian School. The elevation of Murree averages about 7,500 feet, and it gets a lot of snow in winter. There had been a heavy snowfall the night before we went, so Don had to drive very carefully; but at the same time, he had to keep up speed to avoid getting stuck. This was a new experience for me. At times I held tightly to the dashboard, as the van skidded a bit here and there. Yet in spite of my initial apprehension, I was finally able to enjoy the beauty of vast amounts of clean white snow, the likes of which I had never seen before. I was so fascinated by all its beauty that I told Don I wanted to take a large tin can full for Zubeda to see. He convinced me it would not be possible, since the snow would melt by the time we would get to Rawalpindi where temperatures at the lower elevation (1800 ft.) were well above freezing.

Lest anyone think my peanut butter equaled commercially made "Jiffy" or "Peter Pan" varieties in America, I am quick to point out a difference or two. I was able to taste various types of peanut butter during my brief visit to America. I observed that:

1. all peanut butter jars are uniform in size
2. oil does not come to the top after the peanut butter sits for many days. It always spreads like butter

3. there is a choice between smooth and chunky peanut butter. I did see one type of peanut butter in America that resembled my product, but it was only sold in what they call "natural food stores."

I was absolutely amazed by the way commercial peanut butter remained homogenized, regardless of how many days it remained in its container. After my product sits several days, oil rises to the top. I thought this was natural, until I was exposed to commercially made peanut butter. Opening a peanut butter container of my product that has been sitting some weeks requires stirring with a butter knife to reconstitute the homogenous effect. Without this added effort, spreading the peanut butter is like trying to spread half-dried putty. It doesn't spread; it breaks into chunks that a person has to dice and then put on a piece of bread the best he can.

No, my product cannot compare with commercially made peanut butter, but foreigners living in Pakistan without access to the better quality product keep coming back for more. Fortunately, my customers never grew tired of it and enjoyed many snacks of Qureshi Peanut Butter on bread or chapattis. Some of the missionary kids liked it so well that they found the commercially made brands in their home countries rather bland. In fact some MKs (missionary kids) home in college asked their parents to bring Qureshi Peanut Butter with them when they went on home assignments. These MKs not only enjoy my product in their home countries, they find it also serves as a good reminder of their childhood days in Pakistan.

A MOVE TO CITY LIFE

In spite of a regular income from the sale of peanut butter, other problems remained. The increased trouble with Zubeda's family made it evident that we should not stay in the village much longer. As soon as was feasible, we went to Rawalpindi, the twin city of Islamabad, in search of a house. I had given Zubeda money to make the purchase, but for some reason she had not taken it with her. When we found a suitable house, I asked Zubeda for the money. She looked at me in surprise and said she didn't have it. This upset me. I got off the *tonga* and telephoned a friend, hoping he could arrange the money, while we were in town. There was no answer.

Why was God allowing this situation? I was puzzled and became angry over the mix-up. However, when I got back on the *tonga*, I apologized to Zubeda for being upset with her. She reciprocated by apologizing for not bringing the money! What a change from what our reactions would have been before God changed our lives! We marveled again at those wonderful changes.

The house we selected was on the edge of Rawalpindi, in an area known as the Ojri Camp. It was also close to the edge of Islamabad. The previous owners of the house were not pleasant folks, so people in the neighborhood were very glad to see them go. The neighbors wanted a change. They could be Muslim, Christian, Hindu, or anything else. Anyone would be better than that family!

As you would expect, it didn't take long before everyone in the area knew a Christian family had moved in. Most had never lived that close to a Christian family before. They were surprised, however, to find that every so often I talked about Jesus. The Christians they had met previously never did that, so people became curious, as I tried to generate interest in the Injeel and to explain forgiveness of sins through Jesus Christ.

Shortly after we moved in, two neighbors came by. One had met me previously and introduced me to his friend. The friend looked at me with a bewildered expression on his face.

"I had heard that a Christian purchased this property." The other neighbor confirmed his previous statement.

"That's correct. This man is a Christian." Again the puzzled neighbor looked me over inquisitively.

"I thought Christians are white folks, but you're darker-skinned like we are."

This gave me an opening to explain that, even though I was a Pakistani and knew the Quran quite well, I had studied the Injeel and learned the reason Jesus Christ had come into the world. I added that I personally had experienced forgiveness of sins through Jesus Christ, and that I knew for certain that when my time to leave this earth came, I would be in heaven. This man shook his head in disbelief that anyone would say something so arrogant. The reason for his disbelief is that Islam never allows its followers to speak assuredly about getting into heaven. It teaches that only on the judgment day will God reveal the ones to be admitted into heaven. Before then, no one—absolutely no one—can know for sure he will go to heaven after he dies.

House Cleaning

As Zubeda and I surveyed the house we had just purchased, we knew a major cleaning job lay ahead. The previous owner had left things in a mess. Before tackling the task, we went to the market to buy basic supplies. By the time we returned, we were shocked to find that the house had been cleaned. A missionary friend, David Davis, had come with others and cleaned the house for us! What a load off our mind! We were now able to settle in and begin living a normal life again. In doing so we established good relationships with our neighbors. Things were looking better for our family than they had for a long time.

Qureshi, Shafeeq, and David Mitchell

As we became accepted in the neighborhood, an illiterate taxi driver, whom I had befriended, gave me three hundred thousand rupees for safekeeping. This man did not know how to operate a bank account, and he did not trust any of his Muslim friends with that much cash. But he had seen in me a person he could trust completely. This arrangement worked out very well, and he was able get money from me whenever needed.

Also during those three years, I had allowed another neighbor to use water from the tap in our courtyard. But the time came when the city water supply was decreased. Since there was not enough water to share any more, I had to tell him he needed to make another arrangement.

This man was a drunkard and also was on drugs. (Yes, even some Muslims have this problem.) He became upset with me, and to vent his frustration, he complained to the neighbors that there was an infidel living in their midst.

They calmly replied, "Yes, we know that. He has already talked to us about the Bible." What a strange turn of events. In spite of this man's attempt to start trouble, the neighbors sided with us. Their lack of cooperation so upset this troublemaker that he went to an *imam* and gave him five hundred rupees to stir up opposition against me. This *imam* knew which ruffians to contact, so a small mob soon formed and marched to our house. When they reached the courtyard door, I met them with some money, thinking they were taking a collection for the mosque, which was a common practice.

Instead of taking the money, they ranted, "And what about that stone on the courtyard wall? Also, you have the name 'Qureshi' under the cross! 'Quresh' is the name of our prophet's clan! It's a great dishonor to our prophet to have the cross above the name of his clan. We will not stand for it!"

I explained that the Quresh clan was idolatrous and had given the prophet Mohammed much trouble in his lifetime. When they heard that explanation, which was new to them, they cooled down. Later, however, they looked for other reasons to cause trouble. The *imam*'s pride was hurt because of this turn of events, so he said he would return after Friday prayers and bring men with him to remove the offensive stone.

"But God…"

Again, God had other plans. Before the appointed time for them to remove the stone with the offensive words, the *imam* was taken to a hospital with appendicitis. The stone remained in its place for all to see.

All Hell Broke Loose

When we moved into the area, we had no idea what was in store for us. The residential area was part of an army camp, but only the military knew the purpose of this "isolated" army ground. After living in our new house for three years, we and everyone else in that neighborhood suddenly learned it had great significance.

April 10, 1988, started as a normal day. Men had come to drill a well in our courtyard. As they were digging, the drill broke, and they informed me that they couldn't finish the work that day. Zubeda had clothes to wash and wanted water right then. (She was in no mood to give thanks for all things, as commanded in Eph. 5:20.) However, she soon was shocked into realizing that certain things are more important than washing clothes.

Only later did we realize how carefully God orchestrated our household that morning. Shafeeq's wife, Helen, had gone to her parents' home with the children. Sameena was in college; Shafeeq had gone to work. What a blessing that God had our family scattered away from home at that time.

None of us residents in that area had any idea we were sitting on a time bomb. We knew it was an army camp, but that was all. Suddenly, very suddenly, all of us realized we were living next door to a very large cache of munitions.

Sometime in the past the army had dug a very deep pit and stacked it full with munitions. This was before houses sprang up in the area. However, as people began building houses, the army never informed the new residents of the danger. All the living quarters made a good cover up that would keep an enemy from suspecting anything. In those days Russia was trying to take over Afghanistan, and Pakistan was aware of the danger this posed to its own territory. The army had stored enough munitions for such an attack.

Zubeda and I were home alone with Shameem when ear-splitting explosions began. Windows shattered, as rockets emerged from the deep pit that was becoming a red-hot inferno. Explosions shook the earth. No one had a clue about what was happening. Everyone panicked. Rockets were flying aimlessly in all directions, destroying many homes.

Details of this munitions storage place were never released, but it became obvious that there was a humongous supply of rockets and various kinds of munitions stored right in our residential area. The army's hidden secret was unexpectedly revealed. The subterfuge had worked well—until all hell broke loose!

The residents were in a quandary. All of them were scared out of their wits. Families were scattered. Had Russian intelligence discovered this cache? Was it an accident? Was Pakistan's unremitting enemy, India, involved? Those and other questions remain unanswered to this day, but the effect on that area for miles around was literally "earth shaking."

Total number of blasts? Thirty thousand was a number floating around in newspapers. Only army records could give facts, but they were never revealed. Something or someone had unexpectedly started explosions in that deep vault. After the fire was started, there was a domino effect, as one explosion set off the next. That deep silo became a blazing inferno. Heat generated by the top layer of munitions ignited the next layer. So it continued sporadically, layer after layer, explosion after explosion, over a period of five days. Rockets and mortar shells streaked self-propelled across the skies in all directions and randomly damaged buildings for miles around. Fortunately, warheads were not loaded!

As the blasts continued, one after another, I went up on the veranda roof to see what was happening and saw a cloud of smoke at least a mile high above the Ojri Camp. Acrid smoke was filling the air. Rockets were flying off in all directions. One of them knocked out pillars holding the front edge of the roof on which I was standing. Suddenly one side of the concrete slab roof began to sink under me. It was as if large hands were slowly lowering me to the ground. When the outer edge of the roof reached the ground, I stepped off the roof, unharmed, onto the courtyard floor. I found a fire in the courtyard and immediately scooped up sand to extinguish the flames. As God protected me during those dangerous moments, a story from the book of Daniel came to mind. It was the story of God's protection of the three Hebrew men in the fiery furnace. Now he was doing it for me!

Discouraged but not downcast

People all around us were wailing. Many were injured; many had died. As I quickly viewed the carnage, the promise in Psalms 91:7 popped into my mind. "Ten thousand shall fall at your right side, but you will not be harmed." I involuntarily burst out in exaltation, "Hallelujah!"

Suddenly I realized Zubeda was nowhere in sight. I frantically ran into the narrow walkway between courtyard walls of the neighborhood, crying out for her and our daughter, Shameem, but the noise of constant blasts prevented my voice from being heard. In the meantime, Zubeda and Shameem were anxiously looking for me. After many tense minutes, we were greatly relieved to find each other alive and well.

Effects of a stray missile

We all sat in a doorway, stunned. Streets and alleyways were littered with debris. No traffic was moving. Many buildings were in ruins; others had escaped unscathed. Many were damaged. Household items were scattered all over the streets and sidewalks. Sameena's school was destroyed, but we soon learned that one of our friends had seen her walking on one of the littered paths and was bringing her home on his bicycle. Several schools had been destroyed. Parents were hysterical, waiting for their children to appear. Children wondered what they would find when they reached their homes.

Qureshi's daughter Sameena

I thought of getting away from that area in case of further explosions, but then realized we needed to stay near the house, so Shafeeq would know where we were. Finally, he arrived safely. His one-room apartment was on fire. A rocket had entered through its outside wall, gone through the room, and exited through another wall. It left total destruction in its wake. Everything that Shafeeq and his new bride owned was destroyed. Everything they had received as wedding gifts was up in smoke: a fridge, bed set, beautiful bedding, jewelry, and clothing. All was gone—but we all were safe! Praise the Lord!

We didn't know when the next explosions would begin, so we started running. As we were running, a voice suddenly spoke to me.

"Why are you running? Where will you go? What makes you think it is any safer up ahead? Have I not always protected you? There is no need for you to be afraid and run."

I shouted a hallelujah and stopped under a tree with Zubeda, Shameem, and Shafeeq. Others were running past us. We encouraged them to join us. "Come under this tree. You will be safe with us. God is protecting us."

Several who joined us were from Pind Sultani and knew we were Christians. Gradually we became a large group. As we waited almost two hours, our family sang praises to God. Finally, the explosions died down. We looked at each other. Not a single person among us was hurt, not one hair of our heads! It was obvious we had divine protection.

At one point in all the confusion, we noticed our Muslim neighbors were in a state of total shock. Usually after some misfortune or accident Muslims and Christians alike cry out, "Hi-ee, hi-ee!" But everyone was so stunned that even this expression of grief and sorrow would not form on their lips. In contrast, members of our family were rejoicing in the safety the Lord provided by shouting.

"Hallelujah. Praise the Lord. Thank you, Jesus." We

could not contain our joy of God's protection in the midst of such destruction. On the other hand, we told those with us under the tree that had we been killed, we knew we would have gone straight to heaven. For once we did not hear the usual Muslim objection that no one can know for certain whether he is going to heaven until after he dies.

✝

During the confusion, no one had any idea what was going on. India and Pakistan had stood toe-to-toe on more than one occasion, fighting over Kashmir. Had they started a war to try to settle the problem once and for all? On the other hand, Russian forces were in Afghanistan with the hope of eventually getting a route to the sea through Pakistan. Were they behind the random spraying of missiles and bombs? Would there be a lull followed by another round of shelling and bombing?

For two days, fires smoldered from piles of bedding in our house. Everything we owned was burned, including what was left of the taxi driver's money that he had entrusted me with. As for ourselves, all we had were the clothes on our backs.

For several days, the army kept all residents out of the area. But after the government began to allow us back in to examine our property, David Mitchell's son, Jonathan, took me on his motorcycle to see the ruins. What wasn't destroyed by the impact of rockets had been burned by fire started from rocket propellant. We even found missile casings and artillery shells in the courtyard well. Everything we owned was destroyed.

Qureshi and David Mitchell

Further effects of stray missiles

Jonathan described a most interesting detail.

"A man approached, as we were assessing the damage. Qureshi recognized him, for he was the one who had led a delegation to Qureshi's house some years ago to demand that Qureshi change his name. He told Qureshi that his name is a Muslim name and that as a Christian he has no right to use it.

"I was uncertain of his intentions, but learned that just a few days earlier he had been one of those who sought protection with Qureshi under the tree. Without hesitation, he told us the reason he and others had sought refuge with Qureshi:

'Many years ago, in Pind Sultani, we saw God protect Qureshi when we tried to burn down his house. We had kerosene and torches and were ready to start the blaze, but God prevented us from doing that. Because we saw God protect him that night, we knew we would be safe with him in this crisis.' With that he left."

✝

The government recompensed those who had lost property. My property loss totaled over seven hundred thousand rupees, but they offered me only three hundred thousand rupees.

When I pointed out that this was recompense for just the house, and that it did not include Shafeeq's loss or the land, the clerk angrily told me, "You are worthy to die. As an infidel you shouldn't even get this much."

I refused the money. When asked why, I angrily walked out and went home to write a newspaper article to describe the insult. After the article was published, they apologized and told me to take the check, with the promise of another check for three hundred thousand rupees that would come later. The promised check never arrived.

We were able to live two months in a house belonging to a Christian brother, Mr. A. D. Bahadur. In addition to this kind man's help, God provided our needs through donations from a variety of sources. Only God could have coordinated all the various means by which our needs were met.

During my efforts to receive compensation from the government, I noticed how greedy people are. When some scallywags in the area saw how much the government was reimbursing for damages, they purposely damaged their houses hoping for a windfall. What a reminder of the truth of Jer. 17:9: "The heart is deceitful above all things and beyond cure. Who can understand it?"

Shafeeq's burned out room

Normal Life Again

Finally, we were able to sell the ruined house near the munitions cache and buy a two-story house in a crowded section of Rawalpindi.

It's hard for readers in the West to picture our "house." A door allowed entrance into a courtyard from a narrow, dirty street that was constantly used by vendors pushing carts and calling out their wares. These voices added to the cacophony of the busy street. During rains, the street was muddy. In dry times, it was dusty. A dirty, open drainage ditch ran along one side of the narrow street where two-way traffic of ubiquitous Suzuki pickups and animal-drawn carts was at times impossible—but never unsolvable!

Word quickly spread that a Christian family had moved in. This angered some; others found it interesting.

One of our new neighbors met me on the street and commented, "I thought all Pakistani Christians were black, but you're wheat-colored like everyone in this area. Tell me, why did you become a Christian?" His question made an opportunity to explain the good news of Jesus Christ.

The interest in and opposition to our family continued to grow. I was grateful that one neighbor took me into his confidence and informed me that some people wanted to force us out. Some thought it was a dishonorable thing for them to have Christians living in their midst. I inquired as to who was instigating this opposition and learned the name of the man. When I contacted the troublemaker, I explained something new to him: the good news of Jesus Christ. He had never heard that message before. So, I explained the basic facts about Jesus Christ: who he is and why he came. I presented Jesus Christ from the Quran, and this approach got his attention. He listened and gradually changed his mind about Christians—and I gained a new friend.

Shafeeq's Cancer

Our son, Shafeeq, and his family moved into an upstairs section of our newly acquired living quarters. He worked as a secretary/typist in the Ministry of Finance office. In that office environment, he smoked cigarettes and drank lots of tea, the national drink of Pakistan. Whether those habits were contributing factors or not, we don't know, but he developed stomach problems. Doctors in a Catholic hospital in Rawalpindi examined him, but they realized he had something beyond their ability to treat. They referred him to the military hospital.

After a week, the military doctors made the diagnosis of cancer. What a shock! Word quickly spread among the Christian community, and many people began praying. Ten students from Zarephath Bible Institute came to our house to pray for him. Never had so many Christians been together in our home, but these students were eager to pray with us in our crisis. In desperation, I also phoned many friends to elicit prayer and ask for advice.

When we learned of Shafeeq's cancer, we were so desperate that we were ready to sell all we had, so we could take Shafeeq to the USA for treatment. We feared having the operation done in any local hospital, even though friends assured us that many local surgeons were very competent and most had been trained in the West.

I was personally acquainted with staff at Bach Christian Hospital (BCH), some eighty miles north of Islamabad. I phoned the surgeon, Dr. Luke Cutherell, to see if he would do the operation. He was hesitant to commit himself, for our family was very close to him. It would be similar to his operating on one of his own family members. He realized the gravity of the situation and told us he wanted time to seek God's direction. After two days, he said he would do it. David Mitchell quickly arranged to take our family to the mission hospital.

We worried, not knowing if we would bring Shafeeq home alive or not. We were in despair, but two sisters in Christ—Khurshid Khan, a Pakistani, and Garnett DeHart, a missionary—sat with Zubeda and other family members during the long operation. Their presence and prayers greatly comforted all of us. Yet in spite of their prayers and words of encouragement, Zubeda was still under a dark cloud. She knew that God was faithful and cared so faithfully for us, but this was her only son. The Lord knew her need for comfort and provided her a vision of moonlight playing on the ripples of a lake. That soothing scene gave her some degree of comfort, and she was able to relax a bit.

The staff at Bach Christian Hospital had also been praying. As I joined them in one of those times of prayer, I had a vision of a cross, with light coming from it onto Dr. Luke's hands. I involuntarily cried out in jubilation, "Hallelujah!" That sign of assurance even encouraged those around me. We were further encouraged as word filtered in from different parts of the world saying many were praying for Shafeeq.

After the five-hour operation, they took Shafeeq to a private room for close observation.

When he woke up from the anesthesia, those around him smiled, as he asked me, "Abboo, have they done the operation yet?"

Dr. Luke found that the cancer had spread far. But God gave healing from the operation, and on the eleventh day post-op, our family welcomed Shafeeq back home in Rawalpindi. Only one word could describe the operation in my mind: *miracle.*

During Shafeeq's stay in the mission hospital, I preached in the men's ward every day. I reminded the men that we spend so much on our bodies that eventually die, but we think so little about our souls that will last forever. I encouraged them to think about where they will spend eternity.

"You should buy a Bible and read it. God's Word is profitable for all people, whether Christian, Muslim, or Hindu."

It was interesting to note the extra attention men in the ward gave when I preached, as compared with their response when one of the Christian staff preached. The patients found it fascinating that I could quote from the Quran and even point out many references to Jesus in the Quran.

As I adopted a Muslim's way of thinking when explaining the Gospel, I remembered Paul's statement that he became all things to all men, that he might win some (1 Cor 9:22). When I stood before them in "Muslim shoes," their ears perked up; helpful conversations with individuals often followed.

TRAVEL ABROAD

In 1991, The Evangelical Alliance Mission (TEAM) prepared a grand celebration for the one hundredth anniversary of its founding. TEAM's board requested that each of TEAM's fields send two of its nationals to the celebration at Bryan University in Dayton, Tennessee.

The leaders of TEAM's Pakistan field quickly decided on the two they would send. One was a young man named Naz. TEAM missionaries had watched him grow up from infancy and knew him well. By this time, he had completed schooling in Pakistan, obtained a seminary degree in Manila, and was serving as a pastor of the Bach Christian Hospital congregation. Following five years of pastoral experience, he would move into a teaching position at Zarephath Bible Institute in Rawalpindi. The other was a man in his mid-seventies who couldn't speak a word of English, but one whom the Lord had used many, many times in unusual circumstances to explain the Good News to many Muslim friends. I was that man.

Naz had traveled internationally and was fluent in English, so we had few problems navigating various airports from Islamabad to Chicago. Dave Davis met us at the O'Hare airport and later showed us a bit of Chicago. It was summer and ladies were not dressed as modestly as ladies in Pakistan.

I took it all in stride, as I viewed the new sights along Lake Shore Drive.

But one observation was so noticeable that I commented, "Women in America don't spend much money on clothes do they?" (I could not believe my ears when later I learned how much a bikini costs!)

I also noticed various signs along highways.

Dave explained one that read, "Five hundred dollars for littering."

"Littering?" I responded. "In Pakistan it's a way of life. When one travels by train, bus, taxi, or car and has fruit peelings or paper that he wants to dispose of, he simply throws them out, regardless of where he is." I further added, "Pakistan would be a very rich country, if it could enforce such a rule!"

Another time, as we were driving near Lake Michigan, I saw something terrible. I was shocked! This was America, yet I saw a man being dragged naked behind a boat! I wondered why they were punishing him.

Why did I think this way? Several years ago in Gujranwala, some forty miles north of Lahore, a man was having a cup of tea, as he reclined at home on his rope bed. After the first cup he reached over to pour another cup from the metal teapot sitting on a small kerosene stove on the dirt floor. The aluminum handle was very hot so after barely lifting the teapot from the stove, he dropped it back on the little stove. In so doing the stove tipped over, kerosene spilled out, and a small fire spread in the room. He automatically tried to protect the Quran that was lying on a small table right next to him. But by the time he picked it up, it had been scorched.

This strict Muslim panicked and ran into the street shouting his repentance, "I've burned the Quran. I've burned the Quran." If the Quran had been burned on purpose, it would be considered blasphemy and worthy of immediate death. But this was accidental, and he wanted everyone to know it.

A crowd soon gathered, but among the confusion and turmoil, all they understood was that this man had burned the Quran. They cared nothing for the reason. In mass protest, they gathered loose bricks lying around and started throwing. Soon he was unconscious. He never revived. Men tied his corpse to a tractor and dragged it around various streets as an example of what happens to anyone who desecrates the Holy Quran. It made the newspapers the next day, complete with gory pictures.

That story was in my mind when I saw a boat dragging a naked man over the waters. If I had seen this strange activity up close, I would have noticed the man being "dragged" was smiling and enjoying himself, and I would have seen that he was wearing a bathing suit. But I knew nothing of bathing suits or water skiing, so my mind quickly turned to the incident I had read about in Pakistan.

The more I saw of life in America, the more insight I gained into what it means for my missionary friends to leave America and adapt to life in Pakistan. I noticed this especially in standards of cleanliness in public places. I also noticed a greater degree of trust and honesty among people than many people in Pakistan exhibit.

†

After Dave Davis acquainted us with American ways for three days, Naz and I joined representatives from many countries at the conference. One person from each country was requested to bring a short greeting from his country. I had the privilege of representing Pakistani Christians working with TEAM. I was dressed in typical Pakistani garb. As I went on stage to be welcomed by TEAM's chairman, Dick Winchell, I greeted him in Urdu and then, with a big smile on my face, handed Mr. Winchell a can of Qureshi Peanut Butter! The Pakistan missionaries broke into applause. After the interview, I gave Mr. Winchell a big Pakistani hug and walked off the stage.

At the end of this busy day, everyone was ready to get to bed. Most were asleep for the night when a midnight call came from Pakistan. Shafeeq had died. He was only forty years old, and had been doing well after the operation. It seems that a drainage tube, which needed daily attention, was not properly handled. As a result, infection set in and probably hastened his death. He left his wife, Helen, and three boys. Shafeeq's youngest was in utero at the time, and was not born until six months after his death.

Pakistani missionaries gathered in my room to break the news, to pray with me, and just to be with me. It was heartbreaking to be away from my only son at such a critical time. The only reason I hesitated about the trip to America was the fear that Shafeeq might die while I was away. But his post-operative progress was so encouraging that I decided I could be away from him for at least two weeks.

With Shafeeq's death, I felt like an isolated island.

"God, why did you allow this to happen to us? You have done so much for us since we began following you. You know I have seven daughters, but only one son. Oh dear God, why this?"

But I eventually had to admit that in God's economy it was time for Shafeeq to go home to be with Jesus. For him, nothing could be better, but for us, it was a tremendous blow.

Yet I prayed, "Oh Lord, not my will, but yours be done."

Arrangements were made for me to get back to Pakistan as soon as possible. Several brothers accompanied me in a van to Atlanta, Georgia, to catch the earliest possible flight. They all stayed with me until my flight left, but my mind was with my family ten thousand miles away. In thinking back, I recall that in my sorrow and confusion I wandered off to places in the airport without any purpose. Fortunately, my friends kept track of me. Had I been on my own, I could have become hopelessly lost in the cavernous walkways of the airport.

God used the time of waiting for my flight for a good purpose. During that time, one of my missionary brothers met a well-dressed Punjabi returning to Pakistan on my flight. When he heard my predicament, he agreed to see that I would catch all the connecting flights.

After a tearful farewell to my missionary brothers, I entered the huge aircraft. A helpful lady showed me to my seat. I put my handbag overhead, as I had learned to do on the flight to America. Then I sat down and buried my head in my hands. Thoughts raced through my mind. One of my greatest sorrows was not seeing my son's face before burial. In Pakistan, burials are done within twenty-four hours. I was certain that Shafeeq's body was already in the ground. Only higher-ups in the military have access to morgues and embalming.

"But God..."

God had a surprise for me! A Muslim military doctor, married to a wonderful Christian lady from Germany, used his influence in a military hospital for Shafeeq's body to be kept in a morgue until I could return. What a wonderful surprise for me when I reached Pakistan. Such an arrangement was not possible for common folks like us.

An Account of Shafeeq's Last Hours

After Shafeeq's funeral, I longed to hear details of his last moments. David Mitchell and his wife, Synnove, were eyewitnesses of those last hours. Here is Synnove's description:

Not too many days after Qureshi left, Dave and I received an urgent call from his family. Shafeeq was in the Civil Hospital and not doing well. "Could we please take him from the Civil Hospital to our mission hospital? If he were there, we are sure he will live."

We immediately went to their house to pick up his mother, Zubeda, his sister, Sameena, and his nephew, Naasar, plus others who could crowd into the covered back of our pickup. We urged Shafeeq's wife, Helen, to go with us, but she needed more time to get her three children ready to go, since they would most probably have to stay in the hospital with Shafeeq for some time. She said she would make her way to the mission hospital on her own.

When we arrived at the Civil Hospital, the family got out and ran into the building. We tried to find a parking spot near the entrance. Our plan was to talk to the family in front of the medical staff to discourage them from moving Shafeeq in his weakened condition. To our horror and total surprise, the family came out with Shafeeq walking and pushing his own IV stand! Even he was convinced that if he could get to the mission hospital, God would heal him! While we stood dazed and not knowing what to do, someone held his IV bag and gave the stand back to the hospital attendants. We couldn't believe our eyes!

With very little help, Shafeeq then crawled into the back of our truck and lay down. His mother, sister, and nephew followed. Zubeda, with her back to the truck cabin, nestled her son's head in her lap. Sameena and Naasar, finding a place on each side of him, prayed softly and began to lovingly massage his lower legs and feet. We tried again, to no avail, to explain that we didn't think Shafeeq could tolerate the two-hour journey over rough, winding roads, but they were not deterred.

After praying that God would touch Shafeeq and give us a safe trip, we reluctantly set out for the mission hospital. We urged members of the family staying behind to phone the mission hospital to let them know the situation, so that the medical staff would be prepared for our arrival.

We chose the shorter route. Even though that road had many potholes, time was the crucial factor. This route also would avoid the heavier traffic on Grand Trunk Road. A short time after taking the China factory turnoff, we heard a banging on the window. We saw that something was wrong and stopped immediately. Shafeeq was struggling to breathe.

"You pray while I try to help him breathe," I whispered to his family while crawling into the back of the truck. Before I could do anything, Shafeeq died quietly in my arms.

In utter shock and anguish, Zubeda cried out using the words of the grieving prophet (Jeremiah 3:16–18).

"Oh God, I am in anguish, he has broken my teeth with gravel; he has made me cower in the dust. And my soul has been rejected from peace; I have forgotten happiness. So I say my strength has perished, and so has my hope from the LORD. Oh God, I trusted you, so how could this happen to our only son? Oh God, Oh God!" She lovingly folded her headscarf, placed it under her son's chin, and tied it on top of his head to prevent his jaw from drooping. Then she carefully closed his eyelids, acknowledging that her son had permanently left to be with his Savior.

There was no reason for us to continue on to BCH. With heavy hearts, we turned around and headed back to Qureshi's house. On the way, we tried to find someplace where we could make a phone call to let people at BCH know what had happened, but on that back road there was no shop or home that had a phone. For this reason, the news didn't reach the mission hospital for several hours. In the meantime, Helen, with her boys, had traveled those eighty miles on a crowded bus and arrived at the hospital on their own. Now, all by herself, she had to face the fact that she was not with her husband when he breathed his last.

In Pakistan, funerals are held within twenty-four hours after death. With Helen, her three sons, and a few other members of the family at the mission hospital eighty miles away, and Qureshi's being in the USA, what could be done? God would have to make a way—and he did! A kind, compassionate, military doctor arranged for the body to be kept in the Military Hospital's refrigerated morgue in Rawalpindi, till Qureshi could return for the funeral and have a last look at his son's face.

Qureshi arrived at the Islamabad airport, tired but so glad to be with family. God gave him strength to bring God's peace and comfort to the grieving and distraught family in spite of his own deep pain and shock. He gathered his immediate family together and tearfully reminded them of God's abundant goodness to their family. Then he began to thank and praise God in fervent prayer. The confusion and wailing that had reigned unchecked was replaced by a hushed reverence, as the patriarch of the family brought them into the presence of the God who had redeemed them and given them life eternal through the death and resurrection of Jesus Christ.

Synnove Mitchell with Qureshi and Zubeda

Shafeeq's funeral was held August 30, 1991, in a big tent on the street just outside our house. Pastors Isaac, Barkat Parvaiz, Daniel Sardar, and William Gill had part in the service. Javaid Bhatti gave the message, and Samuel Saroyia led in prayer. Just before the benediction, I recited, in Pakistani fashion, the twenty stanzas of poetry I had written in Punjabi during the return flight to Pakistan. Punjabi-speaking people were greatly blessed by these thoughts and marveled how I could produce such meaningful poetry in the midst of such sorrow. I could only say that God gave me those thoughts during the long hours we soared through the sky.

During the funeral service, professional cooks were preparing food in a twenty-gallon cauldron. It was full of rice with meat and raisins. A smaller cauldron was full of tasty curry. With that amount of food, we were able to feed the three hundred or so who were present at the funeral.

None of Zubeda's relatives came to the funeral, but this was a small price for her to pay in comparison with the assurance that her only son was now in heaven with God's only Son! We buried him the next morning in a graveyard near the church pastored by Reverend Isaac, but we had an unshakeable assurance that one day, his resurrected body would rise from that grave. Sorrow? Yes indeed, but we did not feel the "sting of death" that people who do not have eternal life in the Lord Jesus Christ experience.

Synnove gives her view of the funeral and following incidents:

It was a glorious, God-honoring funeral. The streets around the Qureshi home were packed with people from far and near, both Christian and non-Christian. All entered into the grief of the loss of the peanut-butter man who had so deeply influenced them. The family grieved— but, as those who had *hope!*

The pressure, grief, and deep disappointment of the past weeks could be ignored no longer. Helen, pregnant with Shafeeq's unborn son and deeply longing for the comfort and understanding of her own family, took her three boys and went to be with her siblings. She felt slighted and could not understand why she had not been informed more quickly about her husband's death. Qureshi, understandably wanting his home to be as much like it was before his son's death, insisted his daughter-in-law return, together with her three sons, and live next door where they had lived when Shafeeq was alive! Culture reinforced the need for her to live close to her in-laws, but she was still very upset and not willing to conform to their wishes.

Due to the strong disagreements on this issue, a rift turned into seething anger and a hot quarrel between Qureshi and Helen's brother. Qureshi, in his natural, pre-conversion life, was known for his hot temper. Even Zubeda related the times he went on top of their flat roofed house and rained down abuse and curses on the people who had provoked him. Fortunately, God had changed all that.

After Qureshi became a follower of the Lord Jesus, fellow villagers and Zubeda's relatives urged her to leave him because of his sacrilege. He had rejected God and Islam, but worst of all he referred to Jesus as God, whereas they understood him to be a mere prophet. Their promptings, however, did not bother Zubeda, because his changed life was making such a powerful impression on her.

Even before she came to know Jesus personally, she answered, "Why should I leave him now? He is a much better husband than before and has stopped swearing and giving abuse. Before he became a Christian he couldn't control his temper, but now he can! No, I'm not leaving him!"

However, when Helen refused to return with her boys to live in close proximity to her in-laws, the old nature Paul mentions in Romans 7:21–25 reared its ugly head. For a brief time he reverted back to "the old Qureshi." The disagreement between him and Helen and her brother provoked him beyond what he could endure on his own. Due to the tragedy of not being with Shafeeq the last precious moments of Shafeeq's life, Qureshi was overcome. How could his daughter-in-law leave? She not only left, she also took his grandsons away as well! Something snapped—and the fruit of the Spirit, especially self-control, vanished from him for the time being!

A few hours later, David and I sensed an urgency to get in our truck and drive to Qureshi's house. We arrived in the area and looked down the narrow street in front of their house. We could hardly believe our eyes! There was Helen's brother, at least six-foot two inches, weighing two hundred pounds, and the short, wiry, one hundred and fifteen-pound Qureshi yelling abuses at each other. Their fists were cocked and ready for action. Her brother looked like a trained boxer; Qureshi, like an enraged banty rooster, prancing back and forth, looking for the best opportunity to start the attack! David jammed on the brakes, flew out the door with the motor still running and yelled to me, "Park the car."

He grabbed Qureshi from behind in a powerful grip. Qureshi responded by pouring all his rage into fighting David. They both landed in the gutter, struggling. Neighbors were leaning over balconies, aghast at the scene. Qureshi's daughter, Sameena, joined "Uncle David" in the gutter to help bring her father under control. Finally, they were able to drag him, kicking and struggling, through the front door.

Moving into a side room they confined him in a chair as members of the family joined the huddle. Qureshi protested at the injustice of all that had happened and even mentioned that terrible abusive language was yelled at him.

At that point David interjected strongly, "Brother, you responded with abuse yourself!"

Outraged, Qureshi shot back, "I did not!"

David looked straight into Qureshi's eyes and said, "Brother, I heard you say those abusive words with my own ears!" Horror crossed Qureshi's face as David's words sank in.

Then he quietly said, "If you say I said those words, then I must have said them." Falling down on his knees and burying his head in David's lap, he began to weep and cry out to God for forgiveness.

The work of forgiveness had begun, but there was still work for God's Spirit to accomplish in Qureshi's heart for healing to be complete. The whole Qureshi family tried, to no avail, to persuade Helen to return together with the boys. They stormed heaven with their prayers, but the heavens "seemed as brass." Helen refused to return to the small apartment she had lived in before Shafeeq's death.

Some months later, David drove the TEAM pastors up to BCH for a united day of prayer. Qureshi went with them. On the return trip back to Rawalpindi, seated between Pastor Daniel and David in the cab of the pickup, Qureshi again brought out his deep grief and anger in Helen's taking his grandsons and moving away. Someone suggested from Romans 15:1 that he take the first step towards reconciliation, since he was older and more mature in the Lord. He vehemently insisted that in no way would he grovel at her feet! Helen was the cause of the problem, she was the one who had to humble herself and come back to where she belonged—in her husband's home!

The Word of God is powerful and can reach deep into the heart where human wisdom is powerless to touch. Pastor Daniel and David covered many areas of Scripture, including the Lord's Prayer, but Qureshi kept insisting on his rights and his honor. However, when the words of Jesus in Luke 6:27 were quoted, the Holy Spirit melted his heart and he began to weep.

"Love your enemies, do good to those who hate you, bless those who curse you, pray for those who mistreat you."

He cried out, "Oh God, forgive me! Helen is not my enemy! If I am to treat an enemy this way, how much more that is the way you want me to treat Helen and her family! Show me how to love Helen, how to do good to her, how to bless her, and how to pray for her!" By the time he finished pouring out his heart, there wasn't a dry eye in the pickup cab! The presence of Jesus had melted the hearts of all three of them!

God answered that prayer of repentance in a most unusual way. A few days after the trip home from the united prayer day, the Qureshi family received the heart wrenching news that Helen's brother-in-law had suddenly died of a heart attack. There had been no warning signs. With hearts filled with compassion, Qureshi and family went to comfort Helen. The anger, bitternes,s and mistrust of the past months evaporated, as Qureshi, together with Helen and her grief-stricken sister, called out to God for the comfort of the Holy Spirit. They shared with Helen's grieving family the comfort God was pouring into them since Shafeeq's going home! Qureshi was learning new depths in the powerful message of God's forgiveness.

As a result of God's work in Qureshi's life, Helen and her three sons moved back to her home with her in-laws. What a beautiful setting for what was about to happen. Their rejoicing knew no bounds, when a short while after returning home with her in-laws, she gave birth to Shafeeq's fourth son!

God controlled even that birth. Had local ladies had their way, this new grandson of mine would not have been born. When the ladies' "gossip club" learned that Helen was pregnant at the time of her husband's death, they strongly suggested that she abort the child.

"You have three sons already, and you have no husband to help raise this one. It makes sense that you have only three to raise by yourself rather than four. Think how hard that will be. Make arrangements to rid yourself of this child before it is born."

When I heard this idea, I went ballistic.

"Never! Never in a thousand years will you have that child aborted. It is a gift of God, just as much as your other three. I absolutely will not allow it. Let those women think as they will, but we, as Christians, will not stoop to killing one of our own babies." With that, the matter was settled, and Helen became the mother of four boys.

When this baby was ten days old, despair again cast a shadow over our family. He developed breathing problems and turned blue. The doctors diagnosed pneumonia and gave little hope they could save the child.

Zubeda heard this and pleaded, "Please try! He is the last one to remind me of my son." The doctors continued with what they thought best—and people prayed! God answered and healed our newborn grandson of pneumonia and other breathing complications. Again we were overjoyed at God's goodness.

By God's grace, from that point on, Shafeeq's sons were protected from further problems. In God's providence, all of his sons had a good education, but best of all, they, too, were followers of Jesus Christ. What a joy they would have been to their father, had he lived to see them grow up.

Sameena and sister in kitchen

FURTHER TESTING AND GROWTH

I usually rode my motorcycle in urban areas and never used a helmet. There are no rules requiring a helmet in Pakistan, and I had never seen the need for one. On my motorcycle, I had weaved in and around cars, busses, and trucks for years in quagmires of traffic, and all without incident, so why should I use one? When I was seventy-two years old, I learned the hard way that accidents do happen—and that they happen quickly and unexpectedly. Toward the end of 1994, I tangled with another motorcycle and took a bad spill, which resulted in a broken leg. My grandson, Naaser, got me to a hospital and was even able to get through the red tape, so a doctor could quickly see me.

The doctor put my leg in a cast, but after some days I realized it was not healing properly. My family took me to a small Christian hospital in Rawalpindi for another opinion. Although this hospital deals primarily with leprosy patients, it had the exact type of staff I needed. Just one glance at an x-ray showed them that the cast had been applied incorrectly. They removed it and applied another. This time the bone began to heal properly. At this hospital was a top-notch German physiotherapist working with the German Brethren Mission. Under her kind and tender supervision, I eventually made a complete recovery.

In the meantime, my daughter, Aqeela, and her husband moved from Lahore to Rawalpindi to help with the extra work of hosting guests. At times of sickness, Pakistani culture demands that friends and relatives visit the patient. This is very comforting to the family and to the patient, but it brings a lot of stress as well. The unwritten hospitality code demands that tea, at the very least, be served to each guest. Fazal reluctantly left his job as a calligrapher at the Christian Publishing House in Lahore, since it was their only source of income. However, he submitted to family responsibilities, since it always takes precedence.

My recovery was slow because of my age, but as I began to heal there was less and less demand for the help Aqeela and Fazal were giving.

This situation left them puzzled about their move, so they questioned, "Did we really make the right decision to leave Lahore and Fazal's job to come and help with Father? In Lahore we were better off. There we had our own rented living quarters, and Fazal had a good job! How can we afford food, clothing, and education for our children here in Rawalpindi?"

"But God…"

God had a plan for them in their new location. Work as a calligrapher was being downsized throughout Pakistan due to the rise of computers. The computer was making printing much faster and more economical than calligraphy done by hand. They eventually realized that had they stayed in Lahore, Fazal would have soon needed another job anyway. They realized only later that God had all that in mind when he led them to Rawalpindi.

What a thrill it was for me when they began to realize for themselves that the Lord Jesus knew all this beforehand and had directed them to make the shift. I also saw their dependence on the Lord increase. What could be more pleasing to God and to us as parents? In their utter dependence on the Lord, they were learning the lesson of John 15:5 that without him they could do nothing.

Zubeda's Unwavering Faith

For nearly seven years, God spared our family from further sorrows. Our grandson, Naaser, whom we had raised, developed into a godly young man. I noticed that he inherited several of my traits in the way he became a leader among both young and old alike. He was also instrumental in keeping our family encouraged during the seven years after Shafeeq's death. We knew he would be the spiritual leader for the next generation of our family, as well as being the key figure for financial security for Zubeda and me in our old age. In Pakistan, we are totally dependent on our children and grandchildren in our later years. We were so proud of him. He was twenty-six years old and engaged to a fine Christian young lady. Things looked bright for him and our entire family.

"But God..."

Again God's plan for our family was different from what we would have chosen. As all Christians must realize, we had to bow to the fact that God is God, and we are not. We were reminded again, in a very difficult way, that God has the right to give and to take away. He has the right to make up families, and He has the right to break up families.

Naaser worked in Peshawar as a CT scan operator in a private doctor's office. One day in the spring of 1998, he went to work, and suddenly he was ushered into the presence of the Lord by a heart attack.

Relatives brought the body to Rawalpindi, and we buried him the next day in the Christian graveyard where Shafeeq is buried.

What a privilege he had! It's a glorious thing when a believer goes to be with Jesus. And Naaser did not have to go through the pains and sufferings of a lingering illness. Perhaps he felt similar to Enoch who "walked with God and was not" (Genesis 5:22). For him, it was a wonderful way to go! But what about our family? Did we look at it this way? Yes and no.

Yes, for we knew without doubt where he went. No, for it was another shock and deep sorrow for us. We had many hopes pinned on Naaser. Without Social Security in Pakistan, the older folk depend on younger family members to care for them. Naaser would have provided such care. *But God* ... had other plans, plans we will never understand, but plans that fit his purposes—and that's what matters!

From our human viewpoint, death is the greatest enemy we will ever face. It leaves deep and lasting scars. But in the midst of such sorrow, God gave Zubeda and me a wonderful grip on the assurance of the resurrection. Jesus had defeated death; therefore our family could hold onto his wonderful promise: "Because I live, you also shall live." Relatives and friends again marveled at the amazing strength God gave us as we pointed mourners, Christian and Muslim alike, to Jesus and the power of his resurrection.

Naaser's death provided Muslim relatives and friends a chance to make jabs at our faith in the Lord Jesus Christ. They tried to persuade us to leave such "foolishness" and return to our former religion. Not only that, they also turned the blade inside the wound.

"Why did these two deaths take two much-needed men from your family?" Our Muslim relatives had only one answer, which they screamed at us in many ways, "It is because you left Islam!"

Even one of our daughters, who did not know Jesus as her Savior at the time, responded as one who has no hope. In a delirious state, she screamed at a missionary standing nearby.

"Did Jesus raise Lazarus from the dead or not? If he did, why doesn't he raise Naaser? I'll believe that stuff in the Injeel you talk about—but only if he raises Naaser from the dead too."

With a completely opposite reaction, Zubeda radiated assurance as she replied, "Each and every one of us will die, but where will we be after that? I know where I will be, and I know for certain that my son and now my grandson are in heaven. Neither our daughter nor any of our Muslim relatives can imagine such a wonderful thing!" I was so proud of and thankful for my wife's being such a strong example of a Christian mother and wife!

EPILOGUE

Qureshi's Home Going

Zubeda didn't know it at the time, but she would have to face a more difficult separation within a year. Again she braved the storm, but only in the strength the Lord gave her.

On Tuesday April 13, 1999, at 10:30 in the morning, Qureshi was traveling on his motorcycle, as he had for many years. But that morning, God had other plans for our dear brother. He had another motorcycle accident. This time he didn't survive. After a few days in a hospital, the patriarch of the Qureshi family was gone. At age seventy-six, his time on earth was up. He, too, was in heaven!

It was a shock to his family and to the entire Christian community into which his life had become so vitally entwined. But in the midst of sorrow there was victory and joy. Fellow believers had witnessed his faithful life for the Lord Jesus for years, as he went through many ups and downs.

Many from a Muslim background who have become followers of Jesus Christ find that persecution and opposition are so great that they revert back to Islam. But Qureshi? There was never any doubt about his being a faithful follower of the Lord Jesus Christ. He never turned back, despite of a couple dark episodes in his spiritual life. Therefore, his family knew where he was at the moment he took his last breath. He was in heaven. As stated in 2 Corinthians 5:8, he was "away from the body and at home with the Lord."

At the funeral, there were tears of sorrow, but there also were tears of joy. During his years of following Jesus, Jesus gave him strength to endure whatever he had to face. God's promise in 1 Corinthians 10:13 proved true for Qureshi time and time again:

> No trial has overtaken you that is not faced by others. And God is faithful: he will not let you be tried beyond what you are able to bear, but

with the trial will also provide a way out so that you may be able to endure it.

Zubeda's glorious testimony at the graveside added to the unspeakable joy and assurance everyone shared in the victory of Jesus Christ over sin and the grave.

"I want you to know that I loved my husband very much, but I am so glad that he is home with Jesus, and I look forward to going there too!"

According to Islamic custom in Pakistan, it is unusual for a woman to be at the graveside service. Because of his Muslim background, Qureshi himself discouraged women from attending burial ceremonies. However, he would have been proud and thankful for his wife's words, as his body awaited its final descent into the ground.

After she spoke, men holding ropes gradually lowered the wooden box into the open grave. Others positioned it properly and placed flat stones on earthen shelves carved out on both sides of the grave just above the top of the box. Workers then closed open spaces between the flat slabs with mud. The grave was ready to be filled in. At that point, the pastor led a prayer. After the benediction he leaned over, picked up a handful of dirt, and threw it into the grave. Others followed with handfuls of dirt. Finally, workers with shovels filled the grave and left a pile of dirt the length of the grave. They patted down the dirt with shovels to make two smooth, sloping sides on which people placed flowers. Everyone walked away with this picture of his grave in their minds— their last memory of Qureshi's body.

We will never know on this side of heaven how many people Qureshi pointed to the Lord Jesus. Wherever he went, he talked about Jesus and his infinite sacrifice for our sins. In so doing, he was fulfilling the command of his Lord, "You are to be my witnesses," which means to talk, to tell about Jesus. When talking to Muslims, Qureshi often explained about Jesus that he is mentioned in the Quran. But for any who showed interest, he was quick to bring his listeners to the Bible for the full revelation of who Jesus is and why he came to earth.

None of us can be a Qureshi, but we can use whatever gifts God has given us. How do I compare with Qureshi in witnessing for our Lord? How do you? How many people have you told about Jesus this week? In the past month? In the past year? For Qureshi, telling people about Jesus was normal, a way of life.

His life on earth can be summarized by the words of our Lord Jesus in Rev. 3:8, "You have kept my word and have not denied my name." What a wonderful reception he must have had when entering heaven and hearing the words of commendation from his Savior.

"Well done, good and faithful servant...Enter into the joy of your master."

Life Goes On

After losing the three leading men in their family, the spotlight shifts to Qureshi's faithful wife, Zubeda. Once she became convinced that Jesus is the way to eternal life, she remained a faithful and steadfast witness for him.

Zubeda content with God's provisions

Yes, you did read that she felt God had abandoned her at the death of her only son, Shafeeq. She, too, was still in the flesh, where the old nature raises its ugly head at times. But God didn't leave her there. As promised, he provided her a way of escape from the heartache at losing those three precious men in her life (1 Cor. 10:13).

It is interesting to note the steps in Zubeda's transformation from being a staunch Muslim to being a devoted follower of the Lord Jesus Christ.

1.   Encouraged her husband in his duties as a teacher of Islam.

2.   Endured the rage and anger of a strong-willed and abusive husband.

3.   Discouraged her husband from anything Christian.

4.   Noticed positive changes in Qureshi caused by his reading the Bible.

5.   Began to show interest herself.

6.   Gradually adapted to meeting Christians. (When she first visited a missionary couple along with her husband, she sat isolated in a corner, facing away from the missionary hosts.)

7.   Made the choice to stay with her husband as a Christian rather than leave him to return to the Muslim family in which she was raised.

8. Embraced Jesus and his teachings and followed him in baptism.

9. Eagerly shared with her Muslim neighbors and family the joys of knowing Jesus as her Savior and Lord.

10. Faced death of close family members with steadfast assurance in God's plan.

11. Even into old age and after having a stroke, she maintained joy and assurance in Jesus.

As with any family who has lost a loved one, Qureshi's family has had to carry on with life. His daughter-in-law, Helen, continues living with her sons in a small apartment just next to Zubeda and Sameena. Their relationship has remained solid and sweet.

God has continued to faithfully provide for the family members left behind. They are so grateful that Qureshi was able to purchase the house that provides permanent housing for them. For extra income, they rent out a room on ground level to an industrious man who makes a type of flat bread daily.

God's Unending Faithfulness

A set of concrete steps leads from their courtyard to the living quarters upstairs. As Zubeda aged, she found it very difficult to navigate the steps. Fortunately, it was possible for Zubeda to live in their upstairs apartment days on end without using the stairs. But when she did, several had to help her navigate the steep concrete steps.

Her family took her to a large government hospital in Islamabad to assess the pain in her knees. Doctors informed her that an operation was the only way she would ever overcome her knee trouble. The cost of five thousand to six thousand dollars was prohibitive.

"But God … "

God again intervened and proved himself faithful. This time it was from a most unexpected source. Jonathan Mitchell, son of David and Synnove Mitchell, was living in the US at the time and had a roommate named Jon Coker. Jon had helped support Jonathan's parents in Pakistan for several years and knew the Qureshi family. When he heard about Qureshi's death and Zubeda's need of an operation, he felt God's prompting. He would pay for it!

In 2008, Zubeda's operation was performed in a private hospital in Islamabad by a foreign-trained orthopedic surgeon. It was successful. Zubeda could again walk without the pain she endured for so many years. What a relief for her family to see her walking normally and able to navigate those steep stairs without the excruciating pain she had endured for so long.

On August 25, 2008, Zubeda suffered a stroke soon after she got up in the morning. Fortunately, Sameena was at home with her and took her right away to the International Hospital in Islamabad for treatment. The stroke affected her eyesight and her ability to answers questions. Her arms, hands, and legs all moved, though her left hand was affected. She could recognize the voices of those she knew, and she prayed with understandable words and gave praise to God, as she had done for many years. One visitor gave her the first line of Psalm 23 in Urdu, and she repeated the whole Psalm with only small promptings. Her spiritual life was not paralyzed!

As of 2009, she has regained much of her ability to speak and is able to walk with help. She continues to radiate the love and joy of Jesus. Despite of the loss of a son, a grandson, and her husband, her faith and confidence in the Lord Jesus remains unwavering. She eagerly waits for the day when she, too, will be with them to adore and worship the Lord Jesus throughout eternity, as described in chapters four and five of Revelation.

Zubeda has proven to be as equally strong in the Lord as Qureshi had been. There were even times when she was the stabilizing factor in the family. No wonder Qureshi found Proverbs 18:22 to be an apt description of God's choice for his life's partner: "He who finds a wife finds what is good and receives favor from the Lord."

God alone knew Zubeda was *the* mate for Qureshi. God not only chose and called Qureshi; he chose her, too, not only to be one physically with Qureshi, but also to be one with him spiritually. The Lord Jesus is sovereign and receives all the glory for everything that has happened to and through this dear family.

All of us who are followers of Jesus Christ live in his constant care, as did Qureshi and his family. And we are glad!

To him be all the glory and praise! Amen and Amen!

GLOSSARY

Family Honor: An individual's decisions must agree with that of the enlarged family group on major issues. One of the greatest offenses in this area is if a person leaves Islam. Husbands have had to give up wife and children. Some have lost jobs; some have lost their lives.

Another type of violation of family honor is in the case of an unwed woman, but the point is the same: family honor. A case in point from Bach Christian Hospital. An unwed young lady came in with stomach pains. The medical staff determined she had taken an overdose of pills, because she was pregnant. When the male members of her family discovered this, an older brother took it upon himself to see that she would die for this great family dishonor. The staff tried to convince him it would be better to leave her until the baby was born. They assured him they could provide for her and see that the baby would be adopted by someone. This brother was well educated and presented his case clearly and logically.

"I know you westerners cannot understand our standards. I know that you cannot accept what I will do. I appreciate your interest and willingness to solve the problem. The problem isn't the death, which you will call murder, of my sister and the baby. The problem is the honor of our family. I will take her home and see that the next time she will take enough pills to complete the job." We have no doubt but that he carried through with his plans.

Another unwed pregnant lady came for help, but her family was more understanding, and perhaps less strict in Islamic beliefs. They agreed to leave the young lady, so she could have the baby.

The family told people in their village that their daughter was in the hospital for a large operation. The child was delivered vaginally, so there was no operation scar. The problem was easily solved. The doctor made a minor incision over the abdomen and sewed the incision together. This she could proudly show to the gossiping ladies in the village as proof of her "operation."

Imam: A religious leader who calls the faithful to prayer from the mosque five times each day. He also leads the group of men in daily prayers. At times he gives announcements. On Fridays, he gives a sermon to inspire greater allegiance to Islam. In some areas, he is known as a *maulvi* or *mulana.*

Justice of God: Qureshi's very logical question about the justice of God.

Qureshi's illustration in chapter four is very logical, but it is made without knowledge of the Bible. The Quran teaches that every person is locked in the room and not able to get out to obey God, and that he will be punished for not obeying. Islamic teaching leaves it at that, with the exception of a few whom God might forgive on judgment day.

The Bible provides a way out of the locked room. Everyone in that locked room is spiritually dead, i.e. separated from God. In that condition a person has no hope, for he cannot obey God.

The remedy for death is life. The Bible says those trapped inside the room have access to the key of spiritual life. This frees them from the bondage of the locked room. He who asks Jesus into his heart to forgive all his sins receives eternal life. When a person becomes alive in Christ, he is set free from the locked room and is then able to obey God's commands.

MCS: Murree Christian School, some forty miles north of Islamabad-Rawalpindi. The hill city of Murree lies at an average of seven thousand feet in elevation. During hot summers, the British sent their families to this area to avoid the intense heat of the southern regions.

As more and more missionaries went to Pakistan there was need for a place to educate their children. The Church of England had church buildings and land in the Murree hills. The school board negotiated with the Church of England for the use of some of their property. A large church building was officially deconsecrated, so it could be used for classrooms, a small gym, and offices.

MIK: stands for three words in Urdu meaning "Christian Publishing House." It is has been the source of most of the evangelical books and Gospel tracts in Pakistan.

Ojri: The author's younger daughter was living six miles north of the blasts. A rocket barely missed her house, but went through a concrete wall a few feet away. His son lived in Rawalpindi seven miles south of the blasts. Their double front door was blown open by a nearby explosion from something that landed in their area. The force of that blast bent the heavy bolt holding the two doors together.

Sura: The word used for chapters in the Quran. There are 114 suras in the Quran. The general arrangement is that longer chapters are in the first part of the book and shorter ones towards the end of the book. Each Sura begins with, "In the name of the all-merciful Allah."

TEAM: This an acronym for The Evangelical Alliance Mission, an interdenominational mission with headquarters in Wheaton, IL. As of this writing, they have five hundred to six hundred missionaries serving in various countries.

Tonga: A two-wheeled horse-drawn carriage with a roof over the front and backseats. The seats share a common back. Each seat holds three passengers. The spoked wheels are about four feet high and have protruding hubs that are a bane for other vehicles in cramped traffic.

Urdu: The language of Pakistan. The word "urdu" means an army, because this language is composed of many parts. Urdu is composed mostly of Arabic and Persian words, but also contains English and Sanskrit (an old language of India).

e|LIVE

listen|imagine|view|experience

AUDIO BOOK DOWNLOAD INCLUDED WITH THIS BOOK!

In your hands you hold a complete digital entertainment package. In addition to the paper version, you receive a free download of the audio version of this book. Simply use the code listed below when visiting our website. Once downloaded to your computer, you can listen to the book through your computer's speakers, burn it to an audio CD or save the file to your portable music device (such as Apple's popular iPod) and listen on the go!

How to get your free audio book digital download:

1. Visit www.tatepublishing.com and click on the e|LIVE logo on the home page.
2. Enter the following coupon code:
   62b0-706c-bc85-82c6-b5a3-c93c-4b2a-cac6
3. Download the audio book from your e|LIVE digital locker and begin enjoying your new digital entertainment package today!